Developing Independent Learners

Developing Independent Learners

A Guide for Parents and Teachers to the Student Empowerment Program

Jane C. Wiatr and Mario C. Barbiere

ROWMAN & LITTLEFIELD
Lanham • Boulder • New York • London

Published by Rowman & Littlefield
An imprint of The Rowman & Littlefield Publishing Group, Inc.
4501 Forbes Boulevard, Suite 200, Lanham, Maryland 20706
www.rowman.com

86-90 Paul Street, London EC2A 4NE

Copyright © 2023 by Jane C. Wiatr and Mario C. Barbiere

All rights reserved. No part of this book may be reproduced in any form or by any electronic or mechanical means, including information storage and retrieval systems, without written permission from the publisher, except by a reviewer who may quote passages in a review.

British Library Cataloguing in Publication Information Available

Library of Congress Cataloging-in-Publication Data

Names: Wiatr, Jane C., author. | Barbiere, Mario C., author.
Title: Developing independent learners : a guide for parents and teachers to the student empowerment program / Jane C. Wiatr and Mario C. Barbiere.
Description: Lanham, Maryland : The Rowman & Littlefield Publishing Group, Inc., [2023] | Includes bibliographical references. | Summary: "This book for parents is a step-by-step process in the field of positive behavioral management"— Provided by publisher.
Identifiers: LCCN 2023008078 (print) | LCCN 2023008079 (ebook) | ISBN 9781475871265 (cloth) | ISBN 9781475871272 (paperback) | ISBN 9781475871289 (epub)
Subjects: LCSH: Behavior modification. | Affective education. | Student-centered learning. | Education—Parent participation.
Classification: LCC LB1060.2 .W52 2023 (print) | LCC LB1060.2 (ebook) | DDC 371.39/3—dc23/eng/20230310
LC record available at https://lccn.loc.gov/2023008078
LC ebook record available at https://lccn.loc.gov/2023008079

DEDICATION

Mario

This book is dedicated to my first teachers—my mother and father. My mother insisted I go to college and be the first in the family to have a college degree. I didn't think I was smart enough to go to college, but I listened to her. Years later she encouraged me to go for my doctorate, which, again, I didn't think I was smart enough to achieve, but she was correct. It has taken me decades to learn that sometimes people see and believe in us more than we see and believe in ourselves. Finally, I learned that there are no boundaries to what you can do if you believe in yourself or have someone who believes in you. As educators we never want to extinguish hope, because that may be the only thing children may be holding on to. To all our educators, thank you for what you do, as you really do make a difference.

Jane
To Kyle and Ryan:
I love you to the moon and back!
May you always be happy and healthy and never stop learning. I dedicate this book to both of you for all the times you make me laugh and smile.

Contents

Preface		ix
Introduction		xi
1	Setting the Stage for the Student Empowerment Program©	1
2	Setting the Stage for Mindfulness	7
3	Setting the Stage for a Positive Environment	17
4	Setting the Stage for R #1 Responsibility	37
5	Setting the Stage for R #2 Reflection	45
6	Setting the Stage for R #3 Rules	57
7	Setting the Stage for R #4 Regulation	77
8	Setting the Stage for R #5 Rubrics	87
9	Setting the Stage for the Finale	97
Bibliography		103
About the Authors		107

Preface

Early Childhood Education and the Student Empowerment Program is the result of time, effort, and a collaboration of knowledge, experience, and research dedicated to address the needs of professionals, parents, and caretakers of children. It is also the title of our first book for professionals. When our program is implemented correctly, it easily guides the reader into a step- by-step process and toward outcomes resulting in positive behavior management and success. Our new book, *Developing Independent Learners: A Guide for Parents and Teachers to the Student Enpowerment Program,* is written specifically for parents and caretakers.

Our program uses brain-based research and strategic initiatives to facilitate empowerment in children's cognitive, social, and emotional domains of learning. The first book, whose audience teaches younger children, has been well received by professionals across New Jersey. It is part of a positive cultural change in many schools. Although the focus of our first book is early childhood education, the strategies are appropriate for children of all ages.

This book is co-authored by Jane Wiatr and Mario Barbiere. We have collaborated on all practical and theoretical information presented from cover to cover. We use "we, and I" interchangably, when speaking from our experiences. We wrote this new book with parents and other caretakers in mind, and it outlines how to build self-control and self-regulation in children. For years, the authors have partnered with parents and educators to help them instill self-regulation and self-control and build success. We have instructed parents and educators to encourage self-confidence, self-reliance, and self-motivation in their children and students. Through the implementation of the Student Empowerment Program© and its foundational steps, the 5 Rs©, we have witnessed changes in many classrooms and homes. Both parents and teachers have reported better behavior, improvements in self-esteem, and increases in motivation, with children taking the onus for learning and so much more.

We decided to embark on the challenge of a second publication, simply because parents requested it. From preschool to high school, parents want to be involved with their children. They use many of the traditional strategies that were used by their own parents and learn by searching the Internet in an attempt to discipline well. Unfortunately, parents tell us they have limited success and find only temporary changes riddled with consequences and negativity. As educators, we know that parents are huge influencers in their children's lives, as they are their first teachers. Parents are willing to try again and again to encourage success, build trust, and create a strong rapport with their children. They want to provide boundaries, as well as design a set of clear and concise rules that gain results.

Our program is not typical by any standard. We have worked diligently on the foundational skills that we call the 5 Rs© and have field-tested our program in many homes, classrooms, university symposiums, and workshops. We have received positive feedback from those who implement our program, and we are fulfilling their request of more brain-based information in our new book. We are happy to share our knowledge and expertise with all parents, so that they can "level up" with a fresh outlook on how to discipline their children.

Recognizing what children do well, instead of what they do wrong, is the first step in building self-control and self-regulation. We also encourage parents to share our techniques with their children's teachers. You may find that your child's teacher is using our program or similar strategies and is willing to cooperate with you to implement our behavior program. This will align home and school, thereby building a consistent and strong foundation for learning.

Introduction

Our Student Empowerment Program© is the highlight of our newest book, *Developing Independent Learners: A Guide for Parents and Teachers to the Student Empowermemt Program.* It is a step-by-step process that explains how to develop positive parenting skills, make positive adjustments to your own behavior, as well as your child's, and transform your child into someone who takes the onus for his or her own learning in order to become a self-dependent and regulated person.

From our varied experiences delivering parenting workshops, we have discovered that parents seek resolutions to discipline problems, are open to making changes, desire the need for a peaceful home, and value their child's thoughts and feelings. They wish for their child to be successful in school, have a number of good friends, and be active, healthy, and happy. There have been many times that parents, in the most loving and humble way, have asked us to "fix" their child, assuming that we the professionals have all the answers. Unfortunately, we wish we could say we have all the answers, but we don't. What we do possess is a culmination of many years of experience working with parents and their children and raising our own children; the knowhow to implement structure and boundaries for a child, and the patience to instruct parents while providing them with the education to help themselves.

Our field guide is written specifically with the parent in mind and will provide you strategies and techniques for setting up an atmosphere that is conducive to helping your child gain self-control, self-regulation, and success in learning and life. By picking up this book, you have taken the first step toward the commitment to change.

Chapter One

Setting the Stage for the Student Empowerment Program©

You always pass failure on the way to success.

—Mickey Rooney

The Student Empowerment Program© is a brain-based program that when implemented has proven to be effective in preventing unwanted negative behaviors. It provides the opportunity for parents to focus on the positives, and it explains how to expunge negative, corrective behavioral reactions. The Student Empowerment Program© creates a positive response when one follows the process. The outcomes are apparent when you see a child take a moment to reflect, relax, and regulate his or her mind and body. Mindfulness (chapter 2), and the awareness and attention one gives to the mind, aids in concentration, reflection, learning and regulation.

The components of the program begin with a willingness of parents to commit the time and positive energy required to make a change in the structure of their traditional way of parenting. This change can be slight or great depending on what you wish to change about your current style of parenting.

This book will give you ways to make a change in your discipline methods, as well as in your home climate, culture, language, breathing awareness, self-regulation, and self-control. It will be your responsibility to implement or change parts of the program and tailor them to your own family needs. You are the change agent, and it is up to you to have the stick-with-it-ness to experience a successful implementation.

USE HONEY NOT VINEGAR

You are most likely using some form of behavior modification in your home. Many of the market programs that you can view on the Internet revolve around using negative behavior modification techniques. This means that they have punitive consequences, like taking rewards away, giving checks for poor behavior, and focusing on the negative rather than on the positive things your child *is* doing. Some programs do give rewards, but then take them away if a rule is broken. It is very demeaning to anyone to know that he or she earned something and then lost it, all within the same day.

Some programs and or parents suggest consequences that seem endless such as "grounded for a week." By the time that week is over, the child has forgotten what he or she did wrong in the first place. There are new computer programs that support positive outcomes. Our program, as outlined in this book, focuses on disciplining less and learning more. Learning takes all forms. We are not just speaking of learning in school, but we are speaking about the learning that takes place daily within your home. An out-of-control child cannot learn. An out-of-control parent cannot help "fix" the learning situation.

We start the program with constructing a climate by setting the prevailing mood in the household. This means adults and children align attitudes, set high standards of respect and character education values, and model tone of voice and body language with each other. A negative atmosphere at home can make the environment feel hostile, chaotic, and out of control. A positive atmosphere makes it feels safe, respectful, welcoming, and supportive of all family members.

> *Positive reinforcers are powerful in helping to shape behavior. Natural consequences are learning experiences from making poor decisions and then learning from the mistakes.*

PARENT STRATEGY: DEVELOPING SELF-AWARENESS

Here is an example of how to heighten your awareness of your own perceptions. Please put a rubber band on your wrist and leave it there.

As you read this book, do your daily chores, help your children with homework, cook dinner, watch the news, drive your children to sports or dance class, or any other task you find yourself doing, think about that rubber band. It signifies all your positive and negative thoughts and actions. As long as you have a positive outlook, leave the rubber band on the same wrist where you first slipped it on. If at any time, you find yourself changing your positive outlook to a more negative one, move the rubber band to the other wrist. Why? The answer lies in self-awareness. Ponder these questions as you answer the question why:

- Are you aware that you changed your attitude?
- Was it slight, or did it hit you in the face?
- Did it happen spontaneously?
- Did you try to control it, but lacked the self-regulation to succeed?

You may have quickly decided that your overreactive state of mind and body were not called for, and, at that point, you moved your rubber band back to the original wrist, implying that you can make the necessary changes to a positive outcome. Maybe today the rubber band never moved. Kudos to you! This self-awareness is the driving force behind positive parenting.

Table 1.1: Parent Strategy: Role of Positive Reinforcers vs. Negative Reinforcers

Positive Strategies. (+)	Negative Strategies (-)
Additive —You add something positive.	Subtractive —You take away something or a privilege.
Reinforces positive behavior. Stresses the positive	Reinforces and acknowledges negative behavior. Stresses the "negative"
Reinforces positive behavior	Identifies negative behavior
Reward —positive reinforcement	Punishment —negative reinforcement. Negative reinforcement may not change behavior, but help the person develop strategies to avoid the negative action.
Learning occurs in a safe environment. The person must feel safe to learn.	Punishment teaches fear, which affects learning. Learning is emotional and in an unsafe environment, the person exhibits fear, fight, or flight. It is the brain's mechanism for survival.
Positive reinforcement requires more time to implement and takes longer than negative reinforcement, which is normally prompt.	Punishment teaches fear and obedience to authority, hence its popularity in schools.
Positive reinforcement produces repeated behaviors.	Negative reinforcement solves the problem for the short-term.
Natural consequences result in learning from making mistakes. Behavioral consequences are assigned when learning is necessary by observing the differences in behaviors.	Punitive punishment is demeaning and has no end goal.

FOUNDATIONS OF THE PROGRAM

The next step of the program is the implementation of the foundational *5 Rs©: responsibility, reflection, rules, regulation, and rubrics*. These five steps are the groundwork for the program's skill building. They are the necessary tools for your toolbox. These five areas will help you make significant changes.

PARENT STRATEGY: DEVELOPING YOUR PARENT TOOLBOX USING THE CELL PHONE METAPHOR

Think about your parental toolbox as a cell phone. When you use your cell phone, ask yourself these questions:

- Is my battery charged?
- Do I have good reception?
- Do people want to talk with me, and am I a good listener?
- Can I dial out or just receive calls?
- Do I have my emergency lines ready?
- Are my wires crossed?

Based on your answers, you will begin to construct a personal toolbox for positive corrective behaviors. The 5 Rs© will be in your quality toolbox. Your toolbox will also include information about language development, breathing exercises, mindfulness exercises, family meetings, rule charts, structure, and boundaries. The 5Rs© will be discussed in length in chapters 4 through 8. The final chapter will tie the program and its components together.

PROGRAM GOAL AND SUMMARY

The goal of the Student Empowerment Program© is to change unwanted behaviors, build success, and focus on the positive, not the negative. We will do the following:

1. Outline a step-by-step process.
2. Lay the groundwork for a foundation that will add positivity to the climate of your home.
3. Develop your presence with your child.
4. Change your language, so that you are very positive, clear, and concise.
5. Help you learn how to use language to cause a change.
6. Help you learn to focus your attention on what your child is doing correct, while teaching rules and boundaries in your own household.

7. Discuss empty praise.
8. Address rewards and consequences.
9. Discuss behavior modifications such as the credit system.
10. Introduce rubrics; an assessment tool to help your child work to his or her potential.

Included in your reading are activities which you can implement to enhance the process and brain-based facts to help support your learning.

Chapter Two

Setting the Stage for Mindfulness

> Mindfulness can help people of any age. That's because we become what we think.
>
> —Goldie Hawn

Take a moment to intentionally focus on something positive. Or take a moment and look up to the sky. How do you feel in either case? Potential reactions to something calming is a slower heart rate, the relaxation of your mind and body, and an alignment of your neurological system, as well as your spirit. Many call this *mindfulness*. The feeling of being present in the current situation and not overreactive, but highly sensitive of your surroundings, allows you to calm your emotional, physical, and mental processes—or create a mindful state of being.

Mindfulness does not require a lot of effort. Attempt to build time into your daily schedule and implement the strategies and techniques we outline in this chapter. The sooner your child implements mindfulness at home, the faster he or she will learn what his or her body feels like in various situations, and the sooner your child will begin to understand empowerment and self-regulation. As a parent, modeling mindfulness, reflection, self-control, and self-regulation is the key to a productive and positive home. An out-of-control body is hard to manage, whereas a regulated body is easy to manage. The mindful body of a child, who is regulated, is also ready to learn, perform, and focus.

WHY MINDFULNESS?

Practicing mindfulness in the home will change behaviors, change patterns of thinking, and restart your child's body and mind toward a new positive one on the spot. Your child will learn to switch "it" off and then on to something more productive and less negative with the ability to implement this strategy. This is a huge step toward your positive behavior-management strategies.

Engaging children in breathing and movement activities helps them become more aware of their bodies and the sensations within their bodies. They become focused on themselves and their environment. This process teaches them how to use their breath to focus their attention and calm themselves. The goal is for children to learn techniques when they need help *regulating* their emotions or behaviors. Remember: The process requires practice, as one cannot do it once and feel the full effect.

BACKGROUND FOR PARENT STRATEGIES

Here is a sample of good practice. These activities will help you create a climate that is reflective, respectful, regulated, and positive. The activities are targeted for elementary through teen aged children. We suggest that eight- to twelve-year-olds follow the directions pretty closely, but you may want to change these exercise slightly (using vocabulary to meet the developmental age of your child), to meet the needs of younger children or older teens. For example, younger children may draw after an experience, whereas older children may lie on their bed, sit in a chair, or "crash" in a beanbag chair. Your goal is that of listening, reflection, awareness of mind and body, and being present in the moment. Given all these elements, good decision making and behavior changes should result from this practice in time.

These strategies are effective ones to begin a mindfulness practice; they are ones that have proven successful and are the most appropriate for at-home implementation.

Parent Strategy 2.1: Mindfulness through Breathing

> *Brain structure and function are altered when an individual is exposed to excessive stress.*

Try this exercise:

- Pre-read numbers 1 through 8.
- Take a deep breath and rate from 1 to 5 (with 1 being the lowest rating and 5 the highest) how you are feeling right now? Write down your rating.
- Proceed.

1. Sit straight up in your chair.
2. Roll your neck twice in a circle, if you can.
3. Fold your hands in your lap.
4. Breathe deep twice; in through the nose and out through the mouth.
5. Count to ten slowly and methodically.
6. Imagine you are standing at the water's edge, with the warm sun and bright blue water surrounding you (mindful imagery).
7. Open your eyes and reflect on how you feel.

Parent Strategy 2.2: Breathing and Attention

> *The attention span of the human brain is getting shorter. We have lost almost four seconds of our attention span in the past fifteen years. This means on average we cannot concentrate on something for more than eight seconds.*

Ask your child to lie on his or her back or sit on a chair, and you do the same. Set a timer for thirty seconds. Ask your child to listen and then discuss what he or she heard. When thirty seconds has ended, ask your child if he or she had difficulty focusing on just the sounds around him or her or if his or her mind wandered to something else. Request that he or she *just* listen to the sounds (You may say "**I need** you to listen *only* to the sounds around you.") Now, set the timer for one minute and ask your child to listen to the sounds. He or she may hear indoor or outdoor sounds, their own breathing, talking in the home, footsteps, and more. When the minute is over, immediately ask your child how he or she feels, not what was heard. Discuss the sense of relaxation and how it differs from the everyday hustle and bustle that happens before or after school, on weekends or during errands and tasks (Note: Is it this hustle and bustle that you are working toward deleting in the household?)

Parent Strategy 2.3: Breathing Techniques

Breathing reduces anxiety and stress.

Here are some breathing techniques for all ages.

- Back-to-back breathing: This is best done with a sibling or a parent. The partners sit back-to-back and breathe with each other.
- Tummy breathing: Lay down on the floor with a stuffed animal on your belly and watch the animal rise and fall as you breathe deeply.
- Elephant breathing: Clasp hands together. As you breathe in, raise your arms over your head. Next, with hands still clasped, breathe out as you lower your hands in front of your body, similar to the way the trunk of an elephant swings.
- Bubble breathing: Hold an imaginary bubble wand and blow through it. Imagine it has happy feelings inside.
- Balloon breathing: Place hands near the sides of the mouth and blow out as if blowing up a balloon. Expand your hands slowly to the sides as the imaginary balloon gets larger.
- Shoulder roll breathing: Raise and lower your shoulders as you breathe in and out.
- Bumble bee breathing: Place pointer fingers on the ears to close the ears off from sound. Next, hum and pretend to be a bumble bee. Hum in slow mantra type sounds.
- Take five: Stretch your hand outward to see five fingers in front of you. With the other hand, start the roller coaster ride from thumb to pinky and back again while breathing slowly and methodically. Count from one to five or hum (a mantra) as you roll back and forth along the web of your fingers.

- Breathe count to eight: Begin by breathing in through the nose and out through the mouth. Count to eight in your head as you proceed. Breathe in one, breathe out two, breathe in three, breathe out four, and so on. Note: If you lose track of your counting, you can begin again, but the goal is to become so relaxed that you forget about the counting.
- Muscle relaxation: In a comfortable position (lying down or sitting in a comfy chair), begin from head to toe and tense and then release muscles or muscle groups in the body. For instance, squeeze your face and then release; lift and tense your shoulders and then relax them; tense your fists and relax; and so on.[1]

Parent Strategy 2.4: Emotional Freedom Technique

Touch is the first sense that a human brain learns to detect.

The Emotional Freedom Technique uses the body's meridians, which are aligned with acupressure techniques. This is another type of mindfulness in which you use self-talk and breathing techniques while massaging or tapping areas of the body. Self-talk is simply talking aloud to affirm a feeling.

The areas of the body are listed below. Next to each area, we have placed suggestions regarding what your child may say while massaging or tapping. Language should be changed to fit the circumstance and or age (developmental level) of the child.

Karate chop. Tap edge of hand with other edge of hand a few times. Breathe.
Eyebrow. Tap over eyebrow. Say: I am thinking of something.
Side of the eye. Say: I am having trouble concentrating.
Under the eye. Say: So many things to think about.
Under the nose. Say: It's OK to feel this way.
Chin. Say: I know I am a great kid.
Collar bone. Say: It's OK to focus right now.
Armpit. Tap the side of ribcage. Say: I am an important member of this family.
Crown of head. Say: I am great. (Tapping, 2018)

When we think about breathing and mindful moments from a neurological point of view with a connection to the brain, we see that when our emotional brain is stressed, our breath is rapid, as is our heart rate. When this happens it's very hard to perform, concentrate, and act appropriately. This "magic" connected breath sends a message to our amygdala, and our amygdala begins to calm. (The amygdala is the part of the brain primarily involved in emotion, memory, and the fight-or-flight response). This message is sent to the frontal cortex and then, and only then, will the child find regulation and control.

IMAGERY AND MINDFULNESS

As you learn to use imagery, you will be able to support your child on trips throughout the universe using his or her imagination. Think about those words: "trips throughout the universe using their imagination." Did you see the imagery in your mind's eye? If you answered yes, you are beginning to discover what imagery is. When you think about something, you formulate thoughts. Those thoughts can be collaborated with pictures or visuals in your own mind, thereby making the whole scene much more real or fantasy-like.

Parent Strategy 2.5: Magic Carpet Rides

> *Create a picture with words and a sensory experience by using imagery of the mind.*

You are going to take your child on a *magic* carpet (towel or rug) journey. The goal is to introduce your child to the concept of imagery. You will lead the first experience, until your child learns the routine, and then he or she can lead a journey for others.

You whisper the words to your child. He or she should respond in a controlled whisper. This too will aid in regulation and controlled voice tone. It also aligns itself with our program language, which will be addressed in a later Chapter Three. Children will need to know the definition of the terms such as *mind's eye, imagination, journey, lift off, breathe,* and so on. This exercise should be no more than five minutes long and can be used as a transitional exercise to gain control and settle down before dinner, clubs, gatherings, or a special event. Later on, and once the child understands reflection and regulation and begins to demonstrate them, this exercise may extend to fifteen to twenty minutes, as the child is in control and experiencing true relaxation as part of the day.

The parent instructs the students in these steps:

"Lie down."
"Take a deep breath."
"Take another deep breath."
"Close your eyes if you wish, and listen to my soft voice count up and down from zero to ten and ten to zero."
[Whisper] "Here we go. Lift off." [Your child may giggle or get excited for lift-off. That is just fine, as you will see you will gain control very shortly after lift-off.]
"OK, we are up and heading for the sky and outer space. Take another deep breath and hold on to your carpets. We are floating, floating, floating . . . so quietly in the sky. Breathe deep and sigh."
"Where are we going today? It's your turn to pick our first stop, and then I will pick the next stop."

Each time you make a stop at a place of choice, stop and ask your child what he or she smells, sees, hears, tastes, and/or feels in their imagination. Remind your child it is not real; it's imaginary and pretend play. You will begin to understand how much you will need to speak to direct the exercise, as you proceed. Excitement is at a minimum, but often your child will take you to your place of work, his or her school, and familiar places like Disney World, which spontaneously creates a bit of excitement. Use the word *breathe* if this begins to happen, and you will gain composure of the experience once again.

By using towels as magic carpets or clouds or even spaceships, you will change the feeling of your guided imagery. Your child will want to participate, so feel free to whisper open-ended questions and include your crew as they participate in the journey. An older child may visualize the day he or she began driving. Your child may see him- or herself on an open road wearing sunglasses and a baseball cap with the sun shining down. Or your child may visualize surfing at the beach, feeling the waves hit his or her face and the water splashing as he or she rides the wave to the shoreline. Corresponding music may be played during visualization if it seems desirable. Use headphones for an even greater experience.

STORYTELLING, POETRY, AND MINDFULNESS

Storytelling is extremely valuable and an effective way to transmit important information and values from one individual or community to the next. Stories that are personal and emotionally compelling engage more of the brain, and thus they are better remembered than simple statements of facts. Telling stories to your children is highly effective, because parents have an emotional bond with their child.

Stories begin with something new and surprising, and suspenseful feelings ensue when the characters are faced with difficulties they must overcome. The characters find these difficulties are due to a failure or crisis in their past. Then the storytelling leads to a climax, in which the characters must look deep inside themselves to overcome the looming crisis (aka problem-solving). Once this transformation occurs, the story resolves itself. This is called the "dynamic arc." Effective movies and videos show us this same pattern. This is an important part of storytelling, as your child learns to control emotions and regulate during the story, thereby increasing comprehension skills, as well. Readings from William Wordsworth and other classical authors are suggested for older children, and we have added one of our favorites from the Shel Silverstein collection at the end of this chapter.

Why Is Poetry Important for Children?

1. Through the venue of poetry, children can dream "what if?" or "what will be?" They can be creative. Children can express themselves through the language used in poetry.
2. Poetry allows a child to develop skills of contemplation and reflection, as they think about the sentences written in a poem.
3. Young children may require explanation and help during poetry readings. They will experience the power of sounds, rhythms, and other patterns within poems while reading aloud.
4. Poetry can help a child improve language development, especially if he or she is able to rewrite the poetry from their interpretation.

5. Poetry expands thinking by encouraging one to see an experience from another perspective.
6. Poetry allows children to break the rules of writing. They are free to write what they wish in order to convey thoughts and feelings. There are no limitations or restrictions while writing poetry.

Parent Strategy 2.6: Imagery in Poetry

> *Your brain has the ability to read someone's face. You may be able to read someone's emotions and feelings just by looking at their face. Your brain is supplying you with the information to judge another's mood.*

I Wandered Lonely as a Cloud[2]
by William Wordsworth
I wandered lonely as a cloud
That floats on high o'er vales and hills,
When all at once I saw a crowd,
A host, of golden daffodils;
Beside the lake, beneath the trees,
Fluttering and dancing in the breeze.

Continuous as the stars that shine
And twinkle on the milky way,
They stretched in never-ending line
Along the margin of a bay:
Ten thousand saw I at a glance,
Tossing their heads in sprightly dance.

The waves beside them danced; but they
Out-did the sparkling waves in glee:
A poet could not but be gay,
In such a jocund company:
I gazed—and gazed—but little thought
What wealth the show to me had brought:

For oft, when on my couch I lie
In vacant or in pensive mood,

They flash upon that inward eye
Which is the bliss of solitude;
And then my heart with pleasure fills,
And dances with the daffodils.

SUMMARY

Mindfulness is the ability to be fully aware of your surroundings, even though you are in a state of deep relaxation. You are present, but not overwhelmed, overreactive, stressed, or anxious (or you are at least less so). Our program advocates the use of mindfulness as part of the daily routine in your household. We explained that scientists have found through brain research that stress and anxiety can trigger the amygdala and neurological system, which respond with the fight-or- flight response. Our goal in this chapter was to explain the benefits of learning transformative techniques and activities, so that you can implement them at home. By learning to breathe and control the neurological system to some degree, the children and adult members of the family will ultimately improve learning, concentration, focus, presence of mind, and so much more. This process will aid in learning self-control and self-regulation. This is also just a good practice for life and a valuable part of the entire program, we have put forth in this book. Also, in the chapter we provided you with examples of storytelling and poetry to add "down time" to your daily routine.

NOTES

1. Retrieved from https://childhood101.com/fun-breathing-exercises-for-kids/.
2. Published in 1807 in *Poems, in Two Volumes*.

Chapter Three

Setting the Stage for a Positive Environment

Shoot for the moon, and if you miss, you will land upon the stars.

—Brian Littrell

"Parents are the children's first teachers." Chances are you have heard this phrase before, and now it is time to apply this concept in a way that helps your child become a lifelong learner and one who develops self-regulatory skills. As you employ the Student Empowerment Program©, you will find the following information valuable, and we encourage you to tailor it to your own parenting situation.

BASIC TIPS FOR PARENTS

Emotions are an important part of learning. Emotional security is an important part of home life. Your child should feel good about his or her environment. Talk to your child about his or her school day, teachers, friends, and the daily happenings of life at school, play, or work. Set aside communication time for this to happen (i.e., dinner, after school), but try not to let a day go by without having this communication. You and your child should make a habit of checking his or her book bag after school as a welcomed routine, and it is also a good time for discussion. After school allows the sharing of information that is fresh on your child's mind. Sometimes children will say, "Nothing happened at school today." To avoid this kind of answer, default to open-ended communication, such as, "Tell me about your day."

If your child describes a tough day, or an unsolved problem, make sure your child knows that he or she can speak with you, and you will listen, as well as help make a plan to solve the problem in a calm, controlled way. Building trust and developing a rapport is crucial. During the tough discussions, remain in a neutral state, as neutrality is the key. This means your body, voice, and mind are all in control of the situation. An overreaction can escalate the situation or bring unwanted negative attention to an already difficult time.

Be aware of the amount of time your child spends watching television, using the phone, video gaming, and sitting in front of a computer. Television shows may be educational, or for enjoyment, but should not replace conversation. Limit television to educational channels or appropriate fun channels by using parental blocks, and limit viewing time to no more than one hour a day.

Authors Betty Hart and Todd Riley's book *Meaningful Differences* describes the value of conversation. Phones should not go to bed with children, and they should be left in a designated area before going to bed, preferably not within your child's arms reach. Blue light from computer and phone screens interferes with sleep, and all screens should be in their own sleep mode for "lights out" time. Gaming may become addictive, and needs to be curtailed before it becomes an obsession. Schedule times for playing video games, as they do have reinforcement and cognitive-function benefits, but limit that time to a couple of hours per week or just weekends, and certainly not before bedtime.

Be aware of your child's diet, as a poor one that lacks essential nutrients may interfere with learning. Aspartame and MSG hamper neurotransmitters in the brain. Research has shown moderation is the key. Eric Jensen discusses nutrition information regarding this topic in his book *The Great Memory*.

Encourage children to attempt homework solo, but certainly guide and facilitate when necessary. Refrain from completing homework for your child, as this does not benefit your child and makes him or her highly dependent on adult support. You may have to sit with your child for a time, until he or she feels secure enough to do the work alone. Always check your child's work after he or she completes it. Do not get angry if he or she makes a mistake, but guide him or her to the correct answer by researching or using open-ended questions or a rubric designed for homework (see Chapter Eight).

If your child's school believes homework is necessary, as some do not, they will tell you that it is a reinforcement of concepts taught during school time. This means your child has "seen and heard" them before. Some new learning may "sink" in, but other new learning may have escaped comprehension. We encourage you to keep on open line of communication with your child's teacher, to discuss your child's progress in school.

For the present, you may encourage a clear and concise understanding of a homework concept by helping your child make "sense and meaning" from the newly taught concept. Use an Internet tutorial, and learn it yourself before working with your child. If you are "lost in the woods," there are usually homework sites given to you by the school, or default to "phone a friend" for help. Staying calm and regulated is the strategy for your child. He or she will see that even when things turn topsy-turvy, you are in control and a problem-solver.

Here is an example of how your child can relearn a school concept at home. Imagine that your child's teacher has assigned the US Constitution review for homework. The teacher has taught and revisited the Constitution at school, yet your child needs reinforcement on the subject. We suggest you use a multisensory approach by reading and rereading the assigned parts of the Constitution with your child. While doing so, make note cards of words, phrases, or events that your child does *not* understand. Together, you can define these concepts on note cards later by using an Internet search engine. These cards will become your child's study cards.

Next, find a video online (for example, "The Articles of the US Constitution" on YouTube) that explains the Constitution in detail. Watch it with your child and explain the necessary content. Good communication is the key to learning, so stop the video and discuss what your child does *not* understand by answering questions and leading a discussion to check for comprehension. Remember, to give positive feedback as you work.

Finally, use a comic-strip project approach to the parts of the Constitution. You may find it fun to draw a picture in a comic strip box of Thomas Jefferson speaking to the Founding Fathers (similar to the mural by Albert Herter titled "The Signing of the American Constitution"), saying "Sign on the dotted line; we can all be Founding Fathers."

When you generate study skills and review comprehension, you build your child's self- esteem. You provide the legwork at home, so your child may reenter the classroom the next day with confidence and not stressed over being "mixed up" about the concept. Sometimes, it's necessary to lay the foundation, as school may move quickly and your child may miss a concept or two. Of course, if you feel the need to speak to your child's teacher regarding the fact that you child is missing the concepts, then do so in a calm and regulated manner.

TIPS FOR STUDYING IN A POSITIVE ENVIRONMENT

Establish a dedicated area for your child to do homework, so it becomes an automatic go-to place. Encourage communication while studying. Talking helps promote the learning process and long-term memory. The person talking internalizes the new concept, because he or she can explain it.

Physical stimulation and oral rehearsal (having your child say aloud what he or she is learning) stimulate the prefrontal (learning) area of the brain. Encourage your child to stand up and stretch or do jumping jacks on occasion. By standing up, a supply of 15 percent more blood is delivered to the brain, and this stimulates the neuron transmitters into learning.

Attempt to connect past learning to *new* learning. Ask your child to connect what he or she is presently studying to what he or she has already learned. For younger children use a chart called KWLH (What you *know*, what you *want* to know, what you *learned*, and *how* you will apply it), or for older children discuss concepts orally, to help stimulate executive function. Transfer of learning occurs when new knowledge is tied to previous knowledge. When applying sense and meaning to a subject, your child will be more apt to learn it and readily retain it. David Sousa's book *How the Brain Learns* has a model for learning with sense and meaning and its importance.

Make sure your child gets enough sleep at night. There is a lot of research on sleep and the sleep cycle (circadian rhythm cycle). A typical four-year-old requires at least nine hours of sleep a night, and a typical high school student requires about eight hours. Get advice from your pediatrician if your child has difficulty falling asleep or has sleep disturbances. Studying or reading a story just before bedtime aids in retention of the subject matter. But blue light from a computer screen can cause disruptions in the sleep cycle, so turn off screens prior to bedtime. Children should *not* take phones to bed, and they should not play video games before bedtime, due to the blue light effect.

Non-learning time has value too. Specifically referred to as "down time," (David Sousa and Eric Jenson: *Teaching with the Brain in Mind*, 2005; *How the Brain Learns*, 2011) because nonlearning time offers time for the brain to make connections. Encourage your child to play outside, chat with family and friends, and have a healthy snack before doing homework. On car rides, talk to your child about what he or she observes, thinks, and feels. Use our guided meditation exercises, imagery, reflection, and mindfulness activities to support your child's down time. (Barbiere, M and Waitr, J (2020) Early Childhood Education and the Student Empowerment Program).

Children have different learning styles. They may be visual, auditory, verbal, physical, logical, social, or solitary. A visual learner likes to use graphs and view materials when working. An auditory learner processes information through listening. A verbal learner uses self talk and recites outloud to learn. A physical learner uses the hands and is literally "hands-on" to perform a task. A logical learner is a mathematician and uses patterns and concepts to learn. A social learner communicates well and learns through speaking to others, and a solitary, or an intrapersonal learner likes to be alone when studying or working. The majority of people, both young and old, are visual learners. Children's differeientated learning patterns are predomonately visual learners. Ask your child's teacher what kind of learner your child is and how you can use that to improve his or her skills while studying.

Reinforce pictures with music. Most learners are visual learners, so pictures are useful for successful learning. Encourage your child to see, hear, feel, or visualize new material. Incorporate auditory and visual learning modalities into your child's learning process. For example, if your child likes to listen to music while studying, play soft background music.

We have used several learning-style inventories in our fieldwork. One such inventory is the Kids Learning Style Survey (ltkcdn.net). An inventory might find that a visual learner requires graphs, posters, or note cards to better understand concepts, while an auditory learner may need to hear a book on tape to fully understand it.

Mnemonics are learning strategies that can be helpful for children. Mnemonics come in many forms, but all are techniques to help a person remember content. Mnemonics may involve using the first letter of words to remember a sequence of events. For example, PEMDAS could stand for "Please Excuse My Dear Aunt Sally," to help a student recall an order of operations in math that includes *p*arentheses, *e*xponents, *m*ultiplication, *d*ivision, *a*ddition, and *s*ubtraction. This mnemonic helps students recall the steps for ordering an algebraic math problem. Mnemonics can also be songs or rhymes to help a student remember subject matter and store it in his or her long-term memory.

Parent Strategy 3.1 Developing a Questionnaire to Set Boundaries

> *Multitasking is bad for performance. Multitasking makes your brain toggle back and forth between several tasks. This causes a drop in attention span, performance, learning, and short-term memory.*

Developing a questionnaire is a good assessment tool for setting boundaries in your household

Parent Questionnaire

1. Do you use sarcasm in the household, either as humor or as a defense?
2. Do you yell or scream to make a point?
3. Does your child talk back to you?
4. Do you have a set of rules?
5. Does your child understand the boundaries?
6. Do you say "no" in an absolute way?
7. Is your self-esteem or your child's self-esteem low?
8. What is your discipline style?
9. Do you "jump" or walk on eggshells to avoid meltdowns?
10. Do you allow your child to fail without "picking" him/her up?
11. Do you have family time?
12. Do you follow a schedule at home?
13. Do you show positive body language when with your child?

14. Does the family or teen overly use social media?
15. Does your child socialize outside of the home?

This questionnaire helps you gather information about you, and in a small, yet significant way, it helps you become aware of interactions, behaviors, and observations of yourself, your family, and the home environment. Questionnaires assess the situation and encourage you to build new pathways to goals and achievements. Here is an in-depth look regarding this questionnaire and why we value them as a family support tool.

Value of the Questionnaire

1. Do you use sarcasm in the household, either as humor or as a defense?

Children under 13 years of age do not understand sarcasm; therefore, it has limited value to the them. Additionally, it does not send a positive message and can be misinterpreted as mean, judgmental, poking fun at someone, and many other negative connotations. Using a positive tone and citing what your child is doing correctly continues to be the most effective strategy when communicating with your child.

2. Do you yell or scream to make a point?

When you respond by yelling or screaming, you have lost control of your emotions and are not presenting your child with a suitable role model to address issues or concerns. Our program teaches self-regulation; we do not advocate yelling, screaming, or punitive consequences.

3. Does your child talk back to you?

It is healthy for a parent and child to dialogue, but it must be done in a respectful manner so the child knows he or she can engage in conversation to resolve problems. The goal for the child is to know that the desirable course of action is the use of words. This expectation is one that should be a rule on your home rule chart. "Use your words" is a great way to state your expectation. It is clear and concise and is the basis for good communication skill building. Sometimes younger children need the words given to them, as they have not experienced a situation and therefore do not know the answer. This is developmentally appropriate, and your best parenting skills are instrumental at this time.

4. Do you have a set of rules?

For a child to understand expectations, he or she must have and understand rules, as rules define boundaries and expectations. If there are no rules or expectations, then everything becomes "negotiable" and often out of control. Without rules, children do not know what, where, when, why, or how "things" flow. What is right and wrong and the correct responses to actions are often overlooked without rules. The phrase *free for all* come to mind when discussing this with parents. Work with your child to establish rules, and set boundaries that are clear and well defined. Rules should be listed with *no* being the first word whenever possible.

5. Does your child understand the boundaries?

Boundaries are a set of limitations that a child uses as a guide to make decisions and choices and solve problems. Once rules and regulations are established, the child will understand boundaries and be able to implement them. Mistakes will happen, but teach your child that mistakes are a learning experience. Always start fresh. Boundaries should be realistic and achievable, because when a child is unable to meet set boundaries it can create undue stress. Boundaries promote reflection and regulation, so boundaries and rules are **must haves** for all parenting styles.

6. Do you say no in an absolute way?

When speaking with children, our voices may not always be definitive. Children sense the tone in which we speak, and they can realize we may not be conveying a sense of truth and/or may not be paying attention to them. They may interpret that we don't mean what we are saying, that we don't really care, or that we don't know how to handle the situation. Sometimes parents can be seen answering nondescriptly, meaning they answer on autopilot. For instance, a child may ask a parent if he or she may have a friend over. The parent responds "no," but does not stop what she is doing, answers with her head in the clouds, and does not address her child face to face. A "no" answer is acceptable, as it is clear and concise, but it should be accompanied by respect, showing the child she is important, as are her words, and that her parent is listening. The parent may choose to give a reason for her "no" response, such as, "We are going out, so there won't be time for friends today, but we can discuss it again tomorrow." Never promise, as broken promises are worse than a "no" to a child. Promises are vague, bottomless, and given to get out of a tight squeeze. What you want to do is speak in an absolute way that clearly defines what the expectations are for your child.

In addition, instead of directing your child to do something, and/ or answering for your child, use questions and open-ended sentences to encourage your child to think about a good solution, or comment regarding the circumstance. You may choose instead to say, "Well, I hear you want a friend over today. We both know we have a full schedule today. Would you check the schedule and let me know if there is time during the day for a friend? If not, see what day on the calendar may be free for this to happen for you." This way you may be able to avoid a "no" response and build collaboration and good thinking between the two of you. "No" is totally acceptable, but should be delivered in a neutral tone of voice followed by a clear and concise parental stand.

7. Is your self-esteem or your child's self-esteem low?

When your self-esteem is high, you handle problems with dignity. When your self-esteem is low, problems become greater and more difficult to address, as frustration and inability to cope are culprits with which to reckon. Parents who feel good about themselves; express love and compassion; are not "controlling" in their parenting style, but open to discussion; are clear and direct in their communication; and are not punitive but strive to build self-regulation and reflection within the family unit are more apt to have children who have a higher self-esteem.

8. What is your discipline style?

There are several ways for parents to discipline their children. The different methods include the following:

Authoritarian: This method involves one-way communication. For example, a parent who is authoritarian may say, "Because I said so." There is no discussion, just a directive that is not to be questioned. This is extremely different from the directive we cited earlier, where the parent is in "neutral" when giving a direction and waiting for a moment to tell the child that he or she did the directive well. The authoritative directive is not neutral; it comes with a harsh, sharp tone of voice and lack of true concern. Children interpret it as, "My parent wants it to be their way or the highway."

Permissive: At the opposite end of the spectrum is the permissive style of discipline. In general, these parents understand that childhood is a journey, so they recognize that children will make mistakes or "act like children," and yes, this is true. But a problem arises when the underlying mindset of the parent is one that places the child as an equal. This mindset lacks boundaries, rules, and regulation.

Uninvolved: Parents who do not invest in most aspects of their children's lives can be said to be an uninvolved parent. Such parents often use discipline randomly without exhibiting a fixed pattern. According to some psychiatrists, this is the worst form of discipline, as it produces low self-esteem, lack of trust, and behavior problems stemming from unclear communication from the parent.

Authoritative: Authoritative discipline is a blend of love and restraint. It is the most preferred discipline style, because it sets boundaries and also delivers discipline in a nurturing way. Authoritative parents set boundaries for their children and also allow them to participate in decisions within those boundaries. Allowing children to participate empowers them as part of the decision-making process. The Student Empowerment Program© and the 5 Rs© are good partners for this type of parenting style.

What Is Your Discipline Style? (indiaparenting.com)

9. Do you "jump" or walk on eggshells to avoid meltdowns?

Learning how to handle your child's or teen's meltdown is important to the outcome of the situation. Meltdowns happen at all ages, from early childhood through adulthood. The trigger or reason that sparked the meltdown provides you with information to develop a successful plan of action. Meltdowns can be the result of anxiety, learning disabilities, neurological issues, sensory issues, hormonal changes, or a normal reaction of a child who is overwhelmed, tired, and/or cranky.

"Shutdowns" are a form of meltdown in which the child escapes into self. These can even be thought of as a quiet meltdown. To learn how to prevent a meltdown, follow these few steps and tailor them to the age of your child—but always default to "breathe."

First, you have to identify the *trigger* for your child's meltdown. A trigger is the thing that sparked the meltdown. Sometimes the trigger is obvious, and other times it is not at all clear. You must be a detective and watch and listen carefully *for the moment* just before the meltdown occurs. That moment contains the reason for the meltdown in many cases. If you can define the trigger, then you can help solve the problem very quickly by simply stating, "We can fix this now, so *take a breath* and let's talk about it right now." If you cannot define the trigger, then begin the next phases of support.

Slide into neutral and ignore the meltdown. When we say ignore, we really mean turn slightly away but remain very aware of your child and carefully watch to make sure he or she is not in any danger or harm's way. You must keep your child safe. This is when you will default to "breathe." If you did not catch the trigger, you will want to begin to work toward the end goal, which is a child with self-control.

While you do all of this, you should also look for the opportunity to use your powerful and supportive words. Your words are very important, as they acknowledge that you see your child is very angry, but moving in way that shows self-control. Start sighting what you see, or what you hope to see, in an attempt to get your child back on the road to recovery.

All these steps happen within seconds of each other. You may decide to say "breathe" immediately, or you may just breathe yourself as you help your child through the tantrum. You have to think on your feet and see what the best fit is for the moment.

If your child rejects your words of support, stop talking and say "breathe" again, staying neutral, and then try again in a few minutes. There is a good chance that you will be able to wait it out, as tantrums are exhausting to the child and he or she will stop and take a break. This is when you will work again to change the direction of the behavior. You may choose to give the credit at this point if you use the credit system. You may say, "I see how well you controlled your screaming. Why am I giving you a ticket?" Wait for the answer, such as "I took a breath and I stopped crying." The less negativity and less attention you give the situation, the faster it will be over. Stay strong and keep your "stickabilty" or stick-to-it-ness.

If your child is having a very long and angry temper tantrum, keep him or her safe, stay in neutral, and wait for the situation to transpire by watching from the corner of your eye. Your child may reject your sightings, so you will need to stop. For the moment, the sighting will be giving attention to the negative behavior, because your child did not take the bait, so to speak. Giving any attention to an out-of-control child is just feeding into the negative behavior. It may be best to just make sure your child is out of harm's way and stay quiet until you actually see him or her calming, and at that moment you can attempt the sightings and proactive work again. This is not easy. We have seen this many times in our work. Keep up the consistency and clarity by following the program, and things will begin to change for you. If you "slip," just start again. Remember: You need to breathe too.

A plethora of resources are available to you, such as pediatricians, child study teams, therapists, social workers, clergymen, earlier bedtimes, healthy foods, and nutrition counseling. There are books, such as this one, that suggest steps to implement a behavioral change when followed fully and consistently.

If as a *parent*, you have the tendency to "melt down," then you should review your role model image (see parenting and discipline question number 10) and plan to make changes in your behavior by seeking out the support you need. Being a role model for your child is a big responsibility. Most influential is how you conduct yourself when you are angry or frustrated, as it serves as a model for your child. Your self-control can serve as a teachable moment. For example, explaining to your child. "I was upset when 'x' occurred, but I stopped and took a breath and then thought about an appropriate course of action and became less frustrated. I decided I am going to do 1, 2, and 3 to remedy the situation. I feel good about this, because I controlled myself and I didn't get frustrated." The child sees that there will be times when others (including parents) get frustrated too, but that they can always work toward a solution. Being a positive role model is every parent's desire, as most parents want the best for their child and their child's happiness. Modeling a positive attitude will show your child that even in times of adversity things will work out.

Finally, continue to work on your action plan and follow it until you reach your goal.

10. Do you allow your child to fail without "picking" him or her up?

A more difficult task as a parent is to allow your child to fail. Your child needs to know that he or she can fail, and from that failure he or she can learn to make changes and ultimately benefit from the experience. Undue "failure" pressure causes a child to quickly give up attempting to become successful. There are many bumps in the road of life's journey, so one must learn how to navigate the highs and lows to be successful. A good parental skill is to allow your child to fail. It's OK to fail. It helps your child learn that he or she can tolerate this emotion, manage the challenge that he or she failed, reflect, reevaluate, and then make a new plan. If your child missed the "opportunity," the concept behind that opportunity will surface again in life, and there is no need for you to clear a path for your child. Don't fall into the trap of making excuses for your child's failure. It's not healthy to "cover" for your child. Instead you can discuss the self-regulation it takes to get through the missed opportunity or failure and how to use our breathing strategy and start again. Defaulting to our program steps is the key to building a new success, a healthy self-esteem, and regulatory skills in your child.

11. Do you have family time?

A family that plays together stays together. Having family time together helps bond relationships and teaches children how to react in a group setting. Children learn to take turns, and they build good communication skills. They learn to lead and learn to follow. They learn to follow directions in games, how to laugh through games, and how to invent their own set of rules for the game. Family time can be unstructured down time or a special trip time. During family time, children observe their parents treating each child in a fair and equal manner, and they learn to understand that *fair* is not always *equal*, as there are different sets of circumstances for each child.

In this lesson children learn tolerance and acceptance, and they learn that it will be "their turn" soon, as their parents treat each family member with great respect and admiration. During family time, and other times, of course, it's important to express your love for your children. They learn they are valued and valuable this way. *Love* is the perfect four-letter word that teaches children a great "how-to" lesson.

12. Do you follow a schedule at home?

There are times when schedules are great and help with predictably, and there are times when schedules overdo life and add stress to situations. Because this book is written to change behavior, we would suggest starting with a daily schedule or a chore chart. This should be just enough to build efficacy and clarify what the expectations are in the home and of your child. Schedules help reduce stress, as long as you don't schedule your child's entire life. Your child deserves unscheduled "down time," as well as knowing that after down time, there is a transition to the next step.

Schedules aid with transitions, or the time in-between, when moving from one activity to the next is when children are the most unsettled. A child may act out for the attention, as the focus is on the transition and not on them. To make this productive, it's important to make your child part of that transition. For instance, at the conclusion of down time, you may direct your child to turn on the lights and come to the kitchen table to do his or her chore for dinner time. Tell your child to do this in a clear, yet neutral tone of voice and wait for him or her to proceed. As he or she begins to complete the directive, "sight" that she has turned the lights on, is working on the table, and setting the tableware in an orderly fashion. You may be more specific in your sighting, depending on how your child responds at this point in your parenting routine.

You will remain with your child at this time, because, remember this is a transition and the "flow of moment" must be steady and productive at the same time. This is especially important if your child has attention deficient disorder (ADD) and/or has difficulty with concentration. With the repetition of schedules, children relax, sleep better, and cooperate in a way that is routine and "neutral," as it is their job to complete the task. This helps children become task oriented, and that aids in completing chores and homework as well. Children with autism do very well with picture schedules, then transition well to picture *and* word schedules, before moving on to all word schedules. Keeping older children with autism on a schedule has shown that they are better prepared for life skills, because of the early intervention of schedules. Overall, you will most likely see a positive change in behavior.

13. Do you show positive body language when with your child?

Positive body language is very important, because one's body language can often supersede his or her verbal language. Children watch your actions, maybe even more then they listen to your words, and you can inadvertently send "messages" with your body that could be interpreted as negative. Positive body language shows your child that he or she is important and that you are interested in what he or she is doing, thinking, or saying. Making eye contact, leaning over or squatting down, or having a posture that shows engagement builds confidence in your child and aids with self-esteem. You want to be cognizant of *not* crossing your arms, turning your back on your child, or hunching your shoulders, as these all express a negative connotation. Our program suggests that during a meltdown, you say "breathe" and slide into neutral, but at other times of the day, you are pleasant, open, willing, and able to use your best and respectful parenting skills.

14. Does the family or teen overly use social media?

Probably the most significant problem facing parents today is "screen time." Children and teens are riveted to their phones, computers, and other electronic devices with little or no regard for how long they are using them. Parents don't know when to put the brakes on and limit their use without the child getting angry or having a meltdown. We default to the rule section of our program, as there should be a written rule about the use of technology when the parent deems it appropriate. Technology may be used for an hour a day, weekends only, or as a reward for positive or change in behavior. It is up to you, how you choose to use it. Writing a rule for technology use on the rule chart might look like this: NO technology on school nights. Or maybe you write "Technology" on the calendar on Friday, Saturday, and Sunday and allow it for one hour each of those days. Finally, you may consider listing it under the reward section of your rule chart (if you are using the credit system) like this: "Technology 15 points = 15 minutes (bonus 5 minutes for not having a meltdown)." Technology also interferes with physical activity and children become "screen potatoes," gaining weight as they snack while on the computer and burn fewer calories than doing something physical like sports. Physical activity is important to promote healthy minds and bodies.

15. Does your child socialize outside the home?

Social skills and socialization with others are important for your child to learn. These skills help your child communicate with others and understand the purpose for this learned communication. Without social skills and socialization, your child could become isolated, and interactions with the outside world can be difficult or stagnant. These skills build a sense of self-worth. They are essential parts of childhood development. You should be intentional with social skills and facilitate the words and gestures your child needs to make successful connections with others. Make sure you "set your child up" for success. If you are attending an outing, give your child time to understand who he or she will be interacting with at your outing. If your child needs help making connections, be supportive, as sometimes younger children need help feeling comfortable with meeting teens or adults. Allowing your child to have choices is important. This means you may say something like, "We are going to meet Dad's family today. You may play with the other children, but if you feel like you need a break, come back over to me." Working with your child in this fashion, will help him or her engage and be more social on his or her own, as each success builds self-esteem, confidence, and the regulation of self.

Building cooperative skills through teamwork is also important, and you can help your child choose a sport that is active or passive in teamwork. For instance, a swim team is collaborative, but the challenge is within oneself, by becoming better with each swim. In contrast, baseball or football are team sports in which everyone works together, and each "play" hinges on a team effort. Either way, building collaboration is important for your child's brain and body to grow and function properly. Encourage playgroups and help your child understand friendship building.

"Although parental involvement has the greatest effect in the early years, its importance to children's educational outcomes continues into the teenage and even adult years. The benefits of parental involvement extend the realm of literacy and educational achievement. Studies show that children whose parents are involved show greater social and emotional development (Allen & Daly, 2002), including more resilience to stress, greater life satisfaction, greater self-direction and self-control, greater social adjustment, greater mental health, more supportive relationships, greater social competence, more positive peer relations, more tolerance, more successful marriages, and fewer delinquent behaviors." (Desforges & Abouchaar, 2003)

The home environment plays a huge role in your child's development and well-being. A home environment that is off-kilter can affect brain development and cause a stress response that may interfere with the child's social and emotional development. Parents who are more likely to combat negative issues with a positive attitude; instill communication, both listening and speaking; discuss feelings; provide rules and boundaries; and set limits will be more successful in supporting the climate of the household. Cooperating and working together, as well as including weekly family time, is so important to the climate of the household.

REFLECTION

In this chapter we have reflected on the overall demeanor or presence of parents and their interactions with their children. We discussed how to instill frequent mindfulness sessions to create an atmosphere that is calm and peaceful.

In addition, we discussed the physical home environment as an important factor in behavioral changes. Any place a child calls "home" should be safe and secure. For some, the home gathering place is the kitchen or family room. It may be a porch or deck in warm weather, where the family comes together to talk, problem solve, and spend quality time playing games, telling stories, or watching a movie. The home has one or more bedrooms where children and adults rest their bodies and minds. The hygiene areas, such as sinks and bathrooms, are equally important to our physical and mental health.

The brain reacts to an unsafe environment in one of three ways: fear, flight, or fight. None is conducive to learning and growing. If the brain feels threatened, it sends a message to the autonomic nervous system, and the body reacts. The brain needs a safe environment and needs to *not* feel threatened for learning to occur. Parents are facilitators of their children's growth and development, and they need to reflect on the value of the good that each person possesses. Parents learn how to draw on that good through the Student Empowerment Program©, so that the climate of the home is positive and one that embraces change in a productive way.

Here is a link to a Bing video that can help further your understanding of the fear, flight, or fight response. In the video, they call it the fight, flight, and freeze responses. Brain Basics: Anxiety (for kids) Part 3 - The fight, flight and freeze responses - YouTube

In this chapter we also wish to address a place that some homes have, and others do not, but we encourage all to consider establishing. We call it the "safe place." It is a space in the house where you can see your child, but it is still semiprivate. It may be full of pillows and blankets or a beanbag chair, or it may contain stress balls or other tools for reducing stress, such as books, headphones, and music. It is a special area where your child can retreat, rest, recoup, restart, and reflect to a better mental and physical place. It is not a punitive punishment area. It does, however, serve as a time-out area, with a pseudo consequence that has positive implications. A safe place is where children (and sometimes grown-ups) can visit to unwind or do a mindfulness or breathing activity to prevent a meltdown or blow up.

THE HOME'S SAFE PLACE

The "safe place" is important to the structure of our discipline program. It allows the child to regain control by implementing the strategies and techniques learned throughout this book. The stimulus/response is almost automatic. In other words, when a parent says, "Breathe," this cues the child to head to the safe place and begin regulatory skills by breathing, counting, doing mindfulness exercises, EFT, and so on. In addition to parental language changes, the safe place is one of the most tried and tested areas of our program to accomplish successful self-regulation. When the child is successful at even the slightest regulation, he or she receives feedback regarding a job well done and sightings from the parent. This success is monumental, as it creates a positive emotional charge. The more successes one has, the easier it is to be successful, as success at changing behavior is a learning curve. We have witnessed children "taking a breath" in their safe place and then on their own merit fully recover from the negative behavior and join the situation at hand once again.

You may also use the safe space before the child loses self-control. It is our hope that with practice in mindfulness and reflection, the child will self-direct and know when a break is necessary, but there will be times when you will tell your child to "breathe" and direct him or her to the safe space. This alone will cut down on disciplining in the household. You will build a success that is not really there by preventing a meltdown from happening. You must be quite perceptive and a keen observer to find that optimum time. You want to secure it before your child loses self-control. With practice, you will be able to see the meltdown coming or realize a trigger just occurred. You may choose to say something like this: "I know this makes you angry, but you can help yourself by taking a break in your safe place. When you are done cooling off, we can discuss your feelings, as they are important to me and I value your input."

Although you aid the process, you leave a direction for the child to take independently: head for the safe space and cool down. You set up the communication to come by inferring it's time for the child to cool down and, once he or she does so, you will discuss—and you make it clear you won't have that discussion while the child is angry. None of those words are uttered, but child knows them through positive repetition and successful encounters with you. This interaction shows the child that he or she will not be punished, that he or she can go cool off, change the existing negative behavior (or at least stop it), and then later will have a chance to express his or her feelings with you, while remaining hopeful that the two of you can obtain a common ground.

With this acknowledgement of success, your child realizes that he or she has made a wise decision to go cool off and reflect on what changes he or she could make to keep his or her behavior regulated. This may require some discussion, but after the cool down time, it's warranted. You will teach rules when they are not broken, which is also known as the best teaching tool for success.

SUMMARY

The parent's positive attitude and the home environment were the focus of this chapter. We reviewed how the parent should review his or her emotions, consider reflection techniques, and implement strategies that lead to positive changes. We provided questions and answers in a questionnaire form for the parent to clarify points that we feel are most important to building an atmosphere that is conducive to growing, learning, and building relationships.

We discussed the importance of emotional security and how to foster an environment that supports feeling safe at home. We suggested such techniques as monitoring your child's diet, screen time, learning environment, homework, and school assignments; using positive reinforcement to get desired results; and setting boundaries. To help set boundaries, we included a questionnaire as a guide for you to follow.

The skills needed to create a positive home environment are the same skills that your child's teacher can use at school, and together you can make a strong home/school connection. When the rules and systems at home are the same as those at school, we find a consistency that makes it easier for your child to establish routines and behave in a manner that is acceptable and successful, and, just as important, your child understands that there is a clear and concise connection between you and the teacher . This speaks volumes in the eyes of the child.

The home as a "safe place" is important to the structure of our discipline program. It allows your child to regain his or her personal regulation and control, by implementing the strategies and techniques learned throughout this book. The stimulus/response is almost automatic.

In the next chapter we will discuss developing responsibility and how to attain it with your child.

Chpater Four

Setting the Stage for R #1 Responsibility

> You cannot hope to build a better world without improving the individuals. To that end, each of us must work for his own improvement and, at the same time, share a general responsibility for all humanity, our particular duty being to aid those to whom we think we can be most useful.
>
> —Marie Curie

As adults, when we think about responsibility, we can easily understand its meaning, because the word has a frame of reference for us. For instance, we are responsible when we arrive to the dentist's office on time. We know that if we are late to the appointment, we would lose our time spot, so we make sure to be responsible and arrive on time. A canceled appointment, due to tardiness, would reflect the consequence of irresponsibility, but the reward of arriving on time is the well-deserved kudos from the receptionist.

When a parent begins teaching responsibility to a young child, the first response from the child may be a quizzical look, as he or she may not understand the meaning of responsibility. However, slowly but surely the child will begin to associate responsible actions with the word the parent presents: *responsibility*.

In the beginning it is important to teach your child that he or she is responsible to complete assigned and expected tasks and be accountable for actions and decisions. The parental goal for your child is to "own his or her action." An example of this would be to tell your child to put his or her books away when finished with them. Then you reinforce your directive by stating, "I see that you put your books away when you where finished reading. Thank you for being responsible." That comment identifies and reinforces positive behavior and defines the action with the word *responsible*. This enables the child to know exactly what he or she did, while making an association to the word *responsible*. When you take the time to carry out this message, you build on the successfulness of good behavior, and increase the likelihood that the behavior will be repeated again, and again.

ALPHA AND BETA COMMANDS TO DEVELOP RESPONSIBILITY

Alpha commands are simple, direct, and explicit to understand, so they can be easily followed. It is important that you don't sound like a dictator when giving them. The word *command* can throw one off, so we suggest you don't use it in your vocabulary. Use the words to make your point. Keep your demeanor neutral, simple, and true to your form. For example, in a calm tone of voice you may say, "Stay put, stop talking, or sit down." When your child follows your words, end it with, "Thank you." It is not necessary to add "please" to the command, as that could sound like you are indecisive to the child. You need to decide for yourself how "please" fits into your requests and sightings about what your child does correctly. Let's practice. Say, "Sit down. Thank you. I see that you did that the first time I asked." Or, "Stay put and stop talking, please. Thanks, I appreciate your cooperation. Boys, you are becoming so responsible. I am so proud of both of you."

Beta commands are often unclear in making a point. Beta commands in general leave a lot of room for interpretation. Depending on the age of the child, and his or her developmental level, a command such as "Let the dog out" may be interpreted as "Let him out, and then leave him out there" for one child, and for another it may mean, "Let the dog out, but monitor the dog's behavior, then let the dog back into the house." In other words, responsibility must be taught and defined specifically for each child. A child will emulate a role model, so it is important that you teach by modeling.

Responsibility, like any other character-education word such as *kindness*, *respect*, and *friendship*, may initially be difficult for your child to understand. Don't take for granted that when you use these words, your child will immediately know how to act. It will require patience and continued reinforcement of practice, examples, and modeling. You may even decide to draw posters of expectations, such as how to support someone. These posters show a desired behavior happening (see examples). The first poster would be applicable for pre-teens and teens, because they already know about supporting a friend, whereas the second poster would be applicable for younger children who are learning to share. The first poster is a good example of humor, not sarcasm.

The second poster shows children holding hands and smiling, and children will most likely interpret it as "support, friendship, sharing, and happiness."

During family time, it may be fun to have your child make a poster that shows examples of support, friendship, happiness, and share with a friend or sibling. Let your child interpret what those concepts mean to him or her and have a family discussion regarding the same. Display the posters in a special place to validate your child's effort.

It is the parents' responsibility to be a positive role model for their children. Responsibility plays a huge part in disciplining, as respect develops out of responsibility to self and others, through the ability to reflect on oneself (see chapter 5). Developing this in a child during the early part of life is important, as it will be apparent when your teen is testing you (a normal stage in a teen's life and one that will require you to default to our program again and again).

I'VE GOT YOUR BACK!

Figure 4.1: I'VE GOT YOUR BACK!

Figure 4.2: I'VE GOT YOUR BACK!

PROMOTING A "PRESENCE OF MIND"

How do we promote the "presence of mind" to teach responsibility and other character and life skills, as well as learn to discipline through nonpunitive measures? First, it is important that you take a moment to think about the following:

1. Am I fully present in the moment?
2. Am I being responsible to the person with whom I am working to make positive changes?
3. Am I using nonverbal cues (i.e., posture, gesture, breathing, tone) in conjunction with my verbal messages?
4. Are my nonverbal messages good ones?

(Remember: Our nonverbal messages may "speak" louder that our verbal messages.)

5. Am I allowing my positive energy to flow through my voice?
6. Do I authentically connect with my child, so that my child understands I am on his or her team?
7. How do I cooperate with others in the family?

The answers to these questions will help you develop a relationship between adult and child that is effective, fruitful, constructive, and valuable. The teen years are particularly hard, as it is the time when the brain is confronting pressures, challenges, stressors, and temptations. The teen brain is still growing and maturing. Teen brains are moving from concrete operations to abstract operations, as Jean Piaget described in his Theory of Cognitive Development. "According to Piaget, the adolescent years are remarkable because youth move beyond the limitations of concrete mental operations, and develop the ability to think in a more abstract manner. Piaget used the term 'formal operations' to describe this new ability."

Lucky for you, the more you teach responsibility, the more you build regulatory skills. It also adds to your positive behavior outlook, which you instill in your child. Both are integral parts of the Student Empowerment Program©. Remember: Our end goal in the Student Empowerment Program© is regulation, self-control, and success of the child *and parent*.

SURVEY 4.1: RESPONSIBILITY SURVEY

> *Located at the front part of the brain, the frontal lobe is responsible for problem-solving, thinking, planning, organizing, short-term memory, movement, motor planning, and personality characteristics.*

DEVELOP A PLAN

After completing the Responsibility Survey, develop a plan of what you will do to make a positive change. For a few days you may want to jot down a record of your responsibilities and include a comment regarding your efforts to make a change. For example:

- I will listen and communicate better.
- I will read the rules and stick to them.
- I will be a good role model.
- I will control my emotions.
- I will default to "breathe."
- I will keep my "stick-with-it-ness."

Responsibility Survey

Score:

5- I need to make a change.

3- I am getting closer and am still working on it.

1- I am terrific at this and happy with myself.

○ a. Self

○ b. Immediate family

○ c. Extended family such as in laws

○ d. Child's teacher

○ e. Child's school i.e. PTA, PTO, if you are a member

○ f. Other professionals like doctor, dentist etc.

○ g. Community

○ h. Job

○ i. Friends

○ j. People in our country

○ k. People in our world

○ l. Planet

Totals: Number of –5's -3's -1's   ○ ○ ○

Reflect: Don't be too hard on yourself. You picked up this book to make changes. This is a simple reflection exercise to help you feel good about how you are improving.

Figure 4.3: Responsibility Survey.

STRATEGIES FOR DEVELOPING A TEMPLATE FOR YOUR PLAN

Remember: You want to be the change you are seeking, and the template is the vehicle for holding yourself accountable. As such, you will first list the task and then evaluate yourself when you complete the task. If you do not accomplish the task yourself, what will you do differently next time?

Table 4.1: Suggested Template

Activity	Strategy	Accomplish the task	If I did not accomplish the task, what next steps will be changed?	Comments

A CHECKLIST FOR DEVELOPING A TEMPLATE

When you begin to fill out the template, and think about how the changes happened or didn't happen, we suggest you first say, "I will start anew right now." Each moment is a new and a fresh moment to begin again. Don't be hard on yourself; making mistakes is a learning opportunity. Here are a few questions to think about:

1. Did I list the activity as one task that can be accomplished, or did I list multiple tasks? Remember: List only one task, so it can be accomplished. If you list multiple activities, it may be overwhelming, and you will get very little accomplished.
2. Did I list proposed strategies that I will use so I can begin doing the task? It is important to have a strategy planned to start the activity. If you don't, you will spend a lot of time planning what to do and may never get to the activity. Think: "Well begun is half done!" Remember: Time is your enemy, so the more you have a plan with strategies, the faster the task will go and the better you will feel.
3. Set time limits, so you are not spending a lot of time on a task. You can use the time as a check-in point to assess your progress.
4. Reflection is the most important aspect for success. If the task did not work out well, be honest in your reflection. The After-Action Review (AAR) is an honest assessment of what worked and what

did not work. There can never be improvement unless you know what needs to be improved.
5. After you make the assessment, think of strategies you can use for the next time you do the task, so that it is more productive.

Feedback is needed for improvement, so in your reflection be honest with yourself. In our next chapter, we will talk about reflection, which will be helpful when you assess your template.

SUMMARY

This chapter was all about responsibility. We all know that unless we are responsible to ourselves and others, we are not going to be productive citizens of our home, city, country, or world. Yes, it can be that global.

Think about the last time you were irresponsible. The opposite of responsible is irresponsible, and we know that the few times we were irresponsible, our task and goals most likely fell apart. We did not accomplish all that we wanted to do, or we let someone else down due to our lack of responsibility. This chapter discusses how you, as a parent, can reflect on your own responsibility and how you will mirror that to your family. Responsibility is the ability to make independent decisions without authority and to be capable of accomplishing actions. With this in mind, you will understand that the first R (Responsibility) is the groundwork for our program.

In this chapter, we included questions to help you view yourself in many areas of life and to learn how to implement changes in a plan of action. We discussed alpha and beta commands and the use of feedback. Without learning responsibility, you will not fully accomplish a positive behavioral management program.

Chapter Five

Setting the Stage for R #2 Reflection

So it's not so much what you reflect on, but how you bring a fresh and abiding awareness to any area of your life that matters.

—Donald Altman, MA, LPC

The process of reflection links a current experience to a previous one. We build new learning, or change old learning that was not considered perfect by the brain. This process involves the brain's frontal cortex and executive brain function, or what is referred to as the *thinking brain*. The brain draws cognitive and emotional information from several sources to evaluate an event. For instance, a sports coach will evaluate the performance of her team after they win or lose a game. If the team loses the game, the coach will determine what needs to be corrected or adjusted to help the team win next time.

The sensory sources that help you reflect and make changes are visual (seeing), auditory (hearing), kinesthetic (moving in space), and tactile (touching), and, of course, we must include tasting. To reflect properly, a person must act on and process the information and synthesize and evaluate the data (or, in other words, think, change or reconstruct, and reflect on that change). In the end, *reflecting* literally means "applying what was learned beyond the original situation."

As a parent, you want to look at yourself (personal reflection) and teach your child how to view him- or herself in his or her "mirror." (Young children may use a real mirror; for older children, the word *mirror* is symbolic of the reflection action.) The mirror concept involves the person acknowledging and evaluating an event by thinking about what he or she sees, thinks, and feels, and by using his or her feelings and five senses. A young child may be instructed to see what he or she looks like when feeling angry. The parent can help teach this by saying, "You are angry. I can see this because your face is very red. Look in the mirror and let's see if we can help you calm down." When discussing this mirror image with an older child, the parent may say, "I can see you're stressed because your fists are clenched. Take some time to breathe, settle into your safe zone, and, when you calm down, we can discuss it. Your thoughts are valuable to me, and later on I will want to hear what you have to say."

During the first part of the conversation, the adult describes exactly what he or she sees in the child's behavior. For example, if a child is disappointed that it is time to leave a friend's home, the parent states exactly what he or she sees in the child's body language and hears in the child's verbal language, how the problem can be solved. Many times a very young child (three or four years of age) cannot problem solve on his or her own, as the senses are overloaded with emotions and feelings. The child may find it difficult to decipher what steps to take to solve a problem. The brain may not have been exposed to this type of problem-solving, or it may be a new learning experience for the child. A positive adult will need to support the child.

Let's think about what we see and hear when a child is disappointed, like the child who didn't want to leave a friend's home. We may witness crying, crankiness, a sad face, holding on to the caretaker's leg, pushing or shoving other children who are in the way, saying no, verbalizing dislikes, or maybe even talking about something that has nothing to do with the issue. The adult should take a neutral stance when learning how to guide a child through the process of early reflection and into the regulation of body and mind. This will help change the behavior and, in the long run, change the behavior to a more appropriate one. We might say to the child, "I see you have a sad face. I can tell that you are not happy. I think you want to stay longer because you love to play here. Am I correct? We can make plans to visit again or even have your friend to our home." The child may react to the positive gentle tone of the adult's voice, and, hopefully, the problem will be solved at this early stage.

If the problem is not solved, the adult should continue by stating, "Although I see your disappointment, I know we can work out a way to fix the problem. I think we should talk about it so you will feel happy again. What did we say we could do?" Assuming the child heard the adult, he or she might say something like, "We can schedule a new date." The adult and child are now solving the problem together.

Of course, you know your child so well that you will be ready to put communication in place before the child has a "meltdown" or temper tantrum about leaving a friend's home. By telling your child that he or she is cooperating and responding the first time you asked, you are building success and laying a foundation for future happy trips to and from any place you may visit.

If you see your child beginning a meltdown or tantrum, intervene as quickly as you can with a "breathe" moment. Say, "Breathe," and then tell your child what you see him or her doing, like controlling his or her emotions (body, language, and so on). Next, do exercises such as EFT (Emotional Freedom Tapping), which you learned in the previous chapter. Your child's friend may choose to participate, thereby supporting his or her friend. This adds a new dimension to the support, as a peer showing acceptance and tolerance for a meltdown is well received by children.

So far we have highlighted younger children, but the goal for a child of any age and his or her parent is to know when to use the "breathe" method, build a success with words, take a moment in the safe zone, if necessary, and then work through the communication between child and parent to problem solve the issue that caused the upset, so that it does not repeat itself in time.

It's important *not* to discuss negative behaviors during the pseudo consequence, aka calming down, breathing, and making the change in your household safe zone. It is very important not to forget you are the role model and should discuss the problem in a civil manner. During this discussion remember the rules and boundaries and keep the conversation factual and objective. Stay in "neutral" with your presence and language, and then affirm your love for each other at the end of the discussion. This rule of thumb is for children of all ages. The mirror reflection becomes innate, with older children able to default to breathing, reflection, communication, and problem-solving.

Self-image is found in the central nervous system. It connects the medial prefrontal cortex, which deals with self-knowledge, to the ventral striatum, which deals with feelings of motivation and reward

Mirror, Mirror

Goal is to recognize feelings and learn to verbalize, problem solve and express feelings appropriately.

Step 1: Parent and child say:

Mirror, mirror on the wall,

I see ...

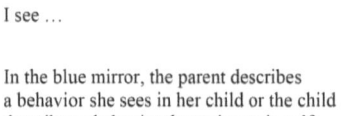

In the blue mirror, the parent describes a behavior she sees in her child or the child describes a behavior they witness in self.

Step 2: Parent guides a child through the process of early reflection and into regulation of body and mind by describing what the child has identified.

Step 3: Parent reflects for her child.

Step 4: The parent uses a plastic mirror (or a real mirror with a good solid plastic support around the outside and a handle to hold) to ask her child what kind of face they would make for happy, sad, etc.

Step 5: The parent asks her child how to correct a negative feeling. When you feel sad, what do you do?

Step 6: When your child is having a problem, follow the mirror and reflection process until the young child is able to verbalize and problem solve without the mirror.

Figure 5.1: Mirror, Mirror.

If the discussion begins to accelerate, then stop and revisit it later. Repeat this pattern until the problem is solved, but don't give in or give up. It must be addressed. It is not going to go away if you ignore it. Sticking to your plan is number one. You, as the parent, will facilitate the problem-solving session. You will keep it on track, keep it positive, and find solutions that work for you and your child. Tell your child all that is good, what you saw him or her do and change, and how you appreciate all her efforts to control her behavior. Mention that this session is to fix the problem and that you will work with together to find a solution that fits best for everyone involved.

The first step in this process is the identification of the problem, not the outburst. *The outburst or meltdown is the side effect.* One must cure the underlying issue with positive changes. All too often we address the side effect and get caught up in the negative behaviors.

This evaluation process, and the use of descriptive sentences, will lead to concrete decision-making and the next course of action. This course of action is the precursor to regulation, and regulation leads to self-dependent learning and positive behavior. Improvement in learning is cited when a child can reflect, predict, and question his or her own learning. Learning is successful when a child puts him- or herself in the pseudo consequence, before an adult says to do so. The child will take a time out, breathe, and regroup. This is the ultimate regulation goal and is a direct result of reflection strategies.

Conflict resolution, problem-solving, communication, critical thinking, and higher-order brain skills are a result of reflection. The goal is to develop self-dependent people who are reflective and regulated and show self-control. This leads to success on all levels.

REFLECTION PROCESS AT HOME

Reflection plays a huge role in a positive climate at home. Reflection is a tool you can use to evaluate a given situation. When the situation is positive, the reflection is a good one and you can express it to the child through lots of positive descriptive language. The more positive language you give, and the more attention to the positive, the more positive responses you will begin to observe. It's a win-win-win. This process continues until your child takes the onus for his or her own behavior, takes breaks on the spot to regroup (or goes to the "breathe" spot until he or she can transition to breathing on the spot to control behaviors), reflects on choices, and gives back descriptive language, for all *you* do that is good as well.

It's not unusual to see a child sit up straight with shoulders back after a parent uses a positive descriptive sentence to note his or her behavior. It is also not unusual to hear a child use the language changes. Children internalize this language, enjoy the kudos they receive from the language, and then use it on their siblings, peers, or adult family members. This is when you know you have a breakthrough moment.

REFLECTIVE EXAMPLES: ACKNOWLEDGE THE POSITIVE

All along this journey of change, you tell your child what he or she is doing like this: "I can see you are ready at the table with your books and pencil. I see you are working so hard on your homework." Or, if you know for a fact that every day your child enters the home and doesn't get ready for homework, then you can choose language like this: "I see you are heading over to the table to begin your homework. That's really commendable, and I am very proud you took the initiative. I didn't even mention it to you. Way to go." This reflects a change in the climate of the household, relationships, experiences, relationship to the child, and more. Just think: *What did I learn and how can I apply it in future?*

Your words may sound different and strange to your child at first, and he or she may laugh, act silly, or question your stability, and he or she may even reject it by ignoring you. Don't stop it. Tell your child you are making a change in your language and it will make your relationship even better. Keep it coming, and soon your child will begin to accept and like it.

REFLECTIVE ACTIVITY: JOURNAL WRITING OR PAINTING

To promote awareness and reflection in your child, you may want to include reflection activities such as journal writing or painting on an easel. For example, journaling may reflect what your child did or experienced over the weekend or on a vacation. You can make a desktop art easel from a heavy box cut into a long rectangle and then folded, so that it creates a trifold tent. Once you have the tent form, tape it to a table or the floor with painter's tape and use a bull clip to hold the paper in place on one side. A stand-up easel is a great way to vertically align the neurological system and get the brain ready to learn. The brain relaxes, de-stresses, and uses problem-solving techniques, as well as cause and effect skills, during this type of experience. Older tweens and teens may find it fun and relaxing to scribble, draw, or use doodle-type art books. A special cover on a journal could make writing in it very special to older children.

Figure 5.2: Tri-fold tent.

RELAXATION ACTIVITY: WHAT DO I OBSERVE?

The smell of chocolate increases brain waves, which trigger relaxation in the brain cells.

A MOMENT FOR ME

In this exercise your child will observe his or her surroundings, which may be a park, beach, home, or any other venue you and your child choose. You will give directions to your child by stating he or she is to name as many details as possible about the surroundings. You will remind your child to use details, which can include colors, shapes, images, smells, textures, sounds, and so on. You will instruct your child to use the senses to develop a writing sample or a piece of artwork regarding the details that have alerted his or her senses. Your child will learn to focus on the sensational experience and begin to appreciate a new way of perceiving the five senses in his or her environment.

It is imperative to help. your child understand how to handle his or her own feelings. This aids in learning how to help your child learn to control and regulate him- or herself. When children are learning about feelings, they can become overwhelmed, and it may be difficult for them to identify the feelings that need to be addressed and in what order they should address them. This type of activity is slow and regulated and allows for critical thinking, classification, and ordering of thoughts.

WHAT IS THE APPROPRIATE RESPONSE?

Responses need to be aligned to the act. Parents often want to use happy and sad faces, but deliberately giving a "sad" face may not be a great choice when there are alternatives. This is different from feeling sad and expressing emotions on a feelings chart or to a family member.

A "dislike tongue and cheek face" could be a good choice, as it keeps it "light and humorous." It is also consistent and clear and may be in line with your own demeanor as a parent who has rules, but also is fun loving. Your child will understand that you do not expect him or her to use this behavior in a real situation. Most importantly, make sure the reasoning behind the emoji is understood. Always think about your charts selections, as they send a message of appropriate or inappropriate responses.

An older child may express his or her like and dislike by using the "two thumbs up method." Two thumbs up is equivalent to a 10 on a scale of 1 to 10. One thumb up is equivalent to a 5 on the same scale, and 0 is a 0 on any scale.

Older students may prefer a number scale with more choices toward decision-making, as shown in Chart 2. The last part of this chart contains a narrative-type reflection. A younger child may need an adult to work with him or her on the narrative, and an older child may work with a sibling, friend, or adult to discuss his or her responses. In addition, some of the responses may lead to deeper communication, such as "I chose the ocean as a 'pass' because when the ocean is calm it's two thumbs up, but when it's rough I would choose pass." The long-term goal is for your child to express his or her emotions and use good (as best as possible) sentence structure to communicate his or her point of view.

> Emotions alter our brains. The chemical reactions stirred by feelings can be seen in brain scans and studies of gray matter. [Huffington Post]

WHY REFLECTION?

The process of reflection is a cycle that needs to be practiced so it becomes second nature. Regrettably, the process is often used when something goes wrong. Why did this happen? What can I do next time? What did I do wrong? All these questions are excellent questions, but the process should be used as a regular course of action. Even if things worked out this time, your one-time success needs to be reviewed and developed to ensure that what worked this time will continue to work in the future.

After you reflect, have your child reflect as well. For instance, if the negative behavior already occurred, you may ask, "What happened just before you did [that]?" Include the action in your case instead of the word *that*. For example, "What were you thinking just before you used foul language?" This will help your child learn to think before her or she acts.

Reflective practice develops your ability to understand how you address problems or challenges and the best ways to address them. By reflecting on your parenting, you identify any barriers you may meet.

After a sports game, a coach reflects on the game, especially if the team lost. The coach begins planning what to do differently next time. Of course, if the team won the game, the reflection process is much more enjoyable. Win or lose, reflection is an important process. When reflecting, use the acronym (mnemonic) DIAR, which stands for *d*o, *i*mplement, *a*ssess, and *r*eflect. The reflection process allows you to link one experience to the next, correcting mistakes and making sure you are making progress.

Make reflection an ongoing part of your daily schedule. Set aside a set time when your child gets together with you, grandparents, aunts and uncles, and family friends to share what he or she has done successfully. A board game, playing cards, or a large puzzle is a good way to learn to relate with your child, to show how important he or she is to you and that you have a strong family unit. Use open-ended questions so you get full-sentence responses, not just a yes or no. This is a good time for family talks and learning to get along with siblings. Eventually, it will be part of the routine.

Chapter Five

Table 5.1: Like/Dislike Chart

Place an X in the box using 1 for the least you enjoy the vegetable, 10 for the most you enjoy the vegetable, and 5 for somewhere in between. Use a 0 if you have never tasted the vegetable.

Name: _____

Vegetable Inventory

Vegetable	1	2	3	4	5	6	7	8	9	10
carrots										
broccoli										
cauliflower										
peas										
turnips										
parsley										
tomatoes										
sweet potatoes										
mushrooms										
bok choy										

It's time to reflect and discuss with a sibling, friend, or adult.

Reflection Questions

Think about these questions as you discuss.

- How did you come to your conclusions?
- How did you order your answers?
- How did you group your vegetables by numbers 1 to 10 or 0?

Setting the Stage for R #2 Reflection 55

Like and Dislike Inventory

This is a template which may be used for classifying activities. This one depicts living things. The categories along the side may be used for anything you wish in order to gather feedback for, i.e., homework, school, assignments, projects, etc

Name: _____ **Living Things Inventory**

	2 thumbs up!	1 thumbs up!	0 thumbs up. I dislike it, but I will use the appropriate face when expressing my dislike.
babies			
doctors			
butterfly			
snakes			
ocean waves			

Reflection: It's time to reflect and discuss your findings with a sibling, friend or adult.

Figure 5.3: Like and Dislike Inventory.

SUMMARY

Reflective practice makes you responsible and your child responsible.

Reflecting on your parenting will help you understand your child's behavior and make him or her accountable for what is implemented in the behavior plan.

Assessing the plan's strengths and weaknesses will enable you to develop an awareness of what needs to be revised, modified, or eliminated.

Reflecting helps to get to the core value of the situation.

Reflecting in a practice promotes your child's ownership of his or her behavior. Giving feedback creates self-awareness and responsibility.

Reflecting on the behavior plan helps your child think more creatively, imaginatively, and resourcefully and helps him or her get ready to adapt to new ways and methods of thinking.

Being reflective helps you challenge your decisions and rationalize your choices.

By getting involved in the reflective process, you and your child will create a partnership that may last a lifetime.

Chapter Six

Setting the Stage for R #3 Rules

You can steer yourself any direction you choose.

—Dr. Seuss

A good behavioral management plan begins with the parent and child formulating a set of rules. The purpose of implementing a behavioral management plan is to define borders, list expectations clearly and concisely, and avoid undefined areas of rule making. It is to enhance positive behavior and work toward the child's ability to successfully follow rules while understanding limits and boundaries.

When we write rules, we want them to be totally understood, so there are no misinterpretations. As adults, we need to explain the definitions of words to older children and define words with actions for younger children. Your child may not understand the difference between words such as *tattling* and *reporting,* therefore, we would first surmise that our rule is not well defined. You may role model what it looks like to report and tattle, and then clarify the difference between the two. Let's further clarify this example.

Reporting is telling an adult that someone is in need. *Tattling* is telling an adult about someone because you want that person to get into trouble. When a child tattles, he or she is attempting to solve intrapersonal problems. When a child reports, he or she has moved into a mature state of mind, relating intrapersonal skills, empathy, concern, and responsibility. The latter is your goal. This is why we surmise that a child may not clearly interpret our definition. Simultaneously, we consider the developmental and intellectual level of the child.

An older child may use the Internet to find definitions with examples or videos of the difference between *reporting* and *tattling*. (Here is a video for your use Tattling vs. Reporting—YouTube). Simple words can make or break the rule, and the outcome can be problematic if the wrong word is chosen. This example should be applied to any word that is not clear to your child.

If parents provide guidance, feedback, and rules written in a positive format as much as possible, the child begins to move away from immature decisions and toward more mature, thought-provoking, and intelligent ones. It is important for the adult to facilitate this crossover from immaturity to maturity and encourage social and emotional behaviors. It is with this support that the child is able to move away from the negative connotation of tattling and go forward toward reporting. This example can be applied to any word that is not clear to your child, using similar techniques and strategies.

HOME RULES

To form boundaries and develop appropriate behavior goals, it is imperative to develop a set of home rules. These rules will reflect changes toward positive parenting. To start, write rules together at a family meeting. Target all that you and your child view as problems. Tell your child and other family members that you have been "observing" and you have seen some great things and some *not* so great things happening in your home. Say, "We are all going to write some rules to keep everyone safe and happy."

Ask, "What are rules?" The answer should be something like this: "A rule helps us remember what is right and what is wrong. Rules keep things in order, just like the supermarket shelves. Rules provide boundaries, and boundaries help us keep our body, mind, and behaviors in good working order. Sometimes rules get broken, and when they do, we can make changes to help make them orderly again." You may need to help with these terms, depending on the age and experience of your child. (Remember our "word" scenario.) Rules represent expected behaviors, management for breaking the rules, expected social interactions and norms, as well as the climate of the household.

A teen already knows the definition of *rules*, so your explanation may be something like this: "We now have written and unwritten rules, because some of our family members are breaking rules, and it is affecting other family members, and that's simply not fair. So, we are going to adhere to the rules, and that will solve our problems." If the teen says he does not see any problems, then you can be more specific and name the rules that are broken by all family members without targeting him specifically, as you do not want to start the program on the defensive.

When everyone is gathered together, ask participants to think about things that need to be changed, either in the home or with them, and write them down. Children and teens are quite good at rule making, although teens will tell you they see nothing wrong. In that case, you lead them into rule making gently and purposefully. They should not judge or attempt to write a rule that changes the behavior or personality of a sibling or adult family member. Each child should write three to five rules in good full sentences (as best as they can) beginning with the word "NO." Remain cognizant that the rules are very clear and concise. Adults should write rules too. We want our rules to be "black and white" with no room for interpretation, which could represent inconsistencies or be misconstrued.

In your rule chart use the word *no* as often as possible. You will want to review the rules, and sometimes they will need to be reviewed daily. If you cannot start your rule with *no*, then find a direct sentence that is clear and specific, such as "Go to bed at 8 p.m." Here are more examples: No hitting; no tattling; report to help others; one person speaks at a time; no interrupting; no fighting; be home at the designated time; put clothes in the laundry basket; and put car keys on the hook daily. It is important to try to use the word *no* as often as possible. Children understand this word, as they use it all the time and see the change it commands. You will not write down some of your rules; we call these "unwritten rules." It's important to include unwritten rules because your child is most likely breaking some rules not listed on the rule chart. This way, you have covered all of your bases, from written to unwritten.

While you are discussing and formulating rules, you are simultaneously teaching the breathing techniques. While you are teaching breathing, you are also teaching reflective strategies and mindfulness throughout your day. Find time in your schedule to add breathing when your child's responses seem to be escalating. Sometimes, just a step back and a breath will help deescalate the situation. Breathing is the key to the self-consequence and your goal in the self-regulation process.

As the family learns to regulate and display self-control, the adults in the family can begin to provide constructive feedback. This feedback will be understood to the child as clear and direct, and he or she will begin to learn that his or her positive actions get positive attention from parents and caretakers. The feedback will come in the form of what we call "sightings." When you see your child conforming, you will say something. You will say things like, "I see that you are making your bed, and your laundry is in the hamper." The focus is on the positive things your child has done, and less on the negative. It will be a weighted-scale example, where the positive will become heavier and the negative will become lighter.

Highlight your sightings with key points from your rule chart. Be aware of your child's reactions as if you had eyes on the back of your head. What we mean is be nonchalant about your observations and keep your comments neutral. You will be providing feedback about what your child is doing well. Sometimes the behaviors you want to address (from the rule chart or unwritten rules) will not be there, so you will "build a success," before a negative behavior occurs. For instance, "You listened the first time I asked." "I see you are working cooperatively with your friend." "You really look like you are serious about making the science experiment work." "I can see you are not giving up on it." "You sat next to your friend when you thought he looked sad." These sentences reflect things that may not be happening to the full extent of your expectations, but to change a behavior you have to build successes when they aren't quite surfacing from the child.

Soon your feedback will become commonplace and will roll off your tongue. It will be part of conversations and you will no longer feel like you are "sighting" all that is good, because the problems will solve themselves when positivity is used in a natural way.

Figure 6.1: Balance Scale.

A COMMON PROBLEM—YOU ARE NOT ALONE

Here's a common problem among parents. Your child often disregards bedtime and stays up reading in the living room until 11 p.m. You have tried to punish by taking away something your child likes, and you have even raised your voice a bit, but to no avail. Your child says, "OK, OK, I am going, I am going," but takes her sweet time getting there. This is when you will employ our method. State: "Our rule is 11 p.m. lights out." That's all you say. When your child makes a move or you have to create an "almost move," you say: "I appreciate how you followed our bedtime rule. You did that the first time I asked." This is quickly stated, there is little talk or effort on your part, no body language or facial expression, and you use a neutral tone of voice. There is no negotiation for extra time to stay up. Extra time to stay up may become a reward down the road, but for now you are steadfast to the rule. The more practice you have and the more success, the more this will become second nature for you.

Note: Some parents and teachers talk too much. They negotiate too much, and they give in too much. What you want to do is talk less, stick to the rules—at least until you get to a point of regulation and maturity, in which time you will be able to negotiate or compromise (by changing the rule to show negotiation and compromising, you will be teaching *freedom* and *independence*, and this is especially important for your teen child). We also don't want to give in to make it go away. It will not go away. The behavior will only escalate the next time, and it will be harder for you in the long run.

Back to the discussion. You may choose to stop here and just allow your child to go to bed. Or you may decide to take it to the next level and give more positives, as you see she really likes the "strokes." So, after noting that she followed the bedtime rule, you may choose to say, "I know you like to read, and so do I. Let's read together on Saturday afternoon. It's a date!" In this case, we guarantee that your child made some type of eye contact with you or an overture toward hearing what you said. Nice work, you got her attention!

The other scenario is that your child does not move. Now it's time to address our "breathe" method. You will learn to use a word that will be equivalent to a pseudo consequence when you do not receive the desired response from your directive. If your child chooses to ignore you, then you will use "breathe" or your word of choice. We like to use *breathe* because everyone does it naturally, and you can easily recognize it and point it out. It also aligns itself with the mindful state and a calm movement forward that we advocate throughout our books.

YOUR SPECIAL DEFAULT WORD

After finding a word to use for this pseudo consequence, discuss it with your family. You will share your expectation for the word when it is spoken aloud. We suggest that when you state your word choice, each family member stand in place and take a breath in order to deescalate incoming negative behavior. You may also instruct your child to retreat to the safe place, where you can still monitor his or her behavior. You may want to practice and role model this while you are discussing it. We have seen parents pretend to be the child and throw a "fake temper tantrum," and when the child uttered the default word, the parent stopped the behavior midstream. When the child used the word *stop*, the parent stopped the tantrum and stood still. Then the child said, "Good job, Mom, you stopped when I said stop."

When you use the word in real time you will begin to see a child who will breathe, stop the unwanted behavior, and change it to a positive one. You will sight this with your words and your positive language. You will also see the child "puff up" from the fact that he or she is noticed by you, when you give the sighting and real-time praise for a consequence well taken. Make sure in the beginning to note how quick that was and how wonderful it is to be able to move forward without incidence.

Finally, you will tell your child that very soon he or she will *not* receive punishments or be given a consequence. *The word* will replace the consequence as the end goal. Explain what your child can expect while he or she is transitioning and getting the program under his or her belt. When your child hears the word one time, he or she should stand in place and change behavior. You may use the word a second time, and a second attempt at standing in place is allowed. If two attempts fail, then for now a consequence is imparted for noncompliance. You will explain at your family meeting that this can be avoided if, as soon as your child hears the word, he or she stands in place and makes a behavior change. Your child will be shocked, very happy, and responsive to no more consequences just for standing quietly.

When we say "for now," we mean that the more times you sight good behaviors and build successes, the less you will have to impart the breathe method down the road. Breathe will become part of your daily routine to show control and regulation in tense situations to control one's self from a meltdown. Punitive consequences will fade with more successes, as it is *not* a goal of this program. The reference to pseudo consequences simply means stopping the behavior, as that is your end goal, and if you continually use positives, rules will be broken less often, and your child will learn to regulate his or her own behaviors.

If you find you need to impart a transitional consequence as you are learning the program, use one that is behavioral. By this we mean that you will impart a consequence that has a "learning" message or one that implies it is a direct result of a rule broken. For example, if your teenage child did not come home on time, with the car you allowed him to borrow, and he was aware of the curfew rule stating 11:00 p.m., then the behavioral consequence would be to remove the car keys, but still allow him to go out to a friend's, driven to and from home by a parent. Of course, he is also to thank the parent for the ride.

Remember to think and reflect upon what went wrong in the first place. Ask yourself, *What is the problem and what is going to be the consequence to match the problem, so that it gets solved next time?* The answer is that he broke a rule and was late. Yes, you were worried, and he has to learn to follow the rules, so that no one has anxiety, no one worries or ends up in a bad situation, and he learns that you will trust him in the future.

Your behavioral consequence is one that is limiting. It imparts to him that time is important and that you will set the control on time, because he could not (this time). You can discuss as a parent the negatives attached to being late. The next time he goes out and gets the car keys, ask him, "What is the rule?" You tell him you trust him and expect him to be home by the 11 p.m. curfew.

We understand that this may be an inconvenience for you, but you are making a point that you have to reteach the 11 p.m. rule and remain in control of your child's actions at this age. Of course, your teenager will not look at this favorably, as he is a teen and is viewed as being chaperoned by his mom or dad (or other adult) in front of his friends. The other choice is that he stay home and serve his consequence through a missed night out. This would be his decision. When you choose to discuss the broken rule, remain in neutral and be very matter of fact in your discussion. Each time the rule is broken, the consequence does not get worse, it is still served in the same fashion and remains consistent.

Show exuberance over the success of his actions when he arrives to your car at 11 p.m. sharp. The next time he follows the rule, again you will sight all that is good with rule following.

Once your child is calm and the moment has passed, move on to another positive, give feedback, and then address the issue that transpired. By all means, if you feel the need to discuss the incident in a parent/child moment, don't let it just go with the pseudo consequence. That's all it takes. Stop the behavior when you hear the default word and we can move on to a discussion to solve the problem. It is very easy for all involved when this program is used consistently.

A TRUE STORY

While teaching school, there was a child who would run down the staircase steps, jump the last three steps to the bottom, and then continue to enter the cafeteria at top speed. He did this for attention and would always watch for my reaction. Upon seeing this, and by asserting a marked increase in new sightings of his good behavior, the staff began to see a huge change in his entry into the cafeteria. All of a sudden, he knew how to walk down the steps, each day making it more refined than the day before. A few more times like this, and he began to see for himself that he was getting attention for proper walking, not jumping steps and entering the cafeteria in a regulated fashion. It worked. This child just wanted attention, and now that he had it, he was entering the cafeteria in a highly appropriate way by walking and using the steps safely.

You are instilling self-control and regulation in your child, and *the word* is creating maturity and responsibility in your child. On occasion, you may tell your child that he or she may be rewarded for listening and making the change. Your reward system will be discussed during the point credit system part of this chapter.

The pay off for all the time you are spending on making sure you sight the positive things, and all the time you spend on great family atmosphere, will ensure that your child will want to be part of this new climate. By remaining neutral and not giving attention to negative behaviors, you are tipping the scale to the positive side and your child will begin seeking positive behaviors over negative behaviors, just like my friend in the story. If your child is young and does not totally understand the concept, he or she will understand the neutrality of the situation and will respond to the word. We have worked with children as young as three, special needs children, and teens and adults, and this program is successful if you make the commitment.

A REAL FAMILY SITUATION

The example here is that of an actual family who had two elementary age brothers. The parents were very positive people, and the positive attributes of our program came easily to them. The parents implemented our program, and after a few months there was no need for consequences. The brothers were able breathe through potential stress and cope by implementing thinking skills and communication. They thoroughly understood their body in "space" and the difference between a controlled body and one that is angry. The parents used the mindfulness, breathing, and reflection techniques. The boys took a pseudo consequence when the parents said "breathe," showing how they could immediately stand in their place and regulate. It took approximately three months to change they boys' behaviors, but the parents did not give up or give in.

These parents learned that life lessons are still required, but *not* when the boys were in a consequence or attempting to control themselves. They used the lesson time after the boys had calmed and were ready to discuss how to solve the problem without anger and meltdowns. The boys are now grown and still respectful and responsible citizens.

This family came up with the following rules, rewards, and consequences:

Rules

Get ready for school
Brush teeth two times a day
Do homework right after school
Put laundry in the hamper
No screaming
Follow screen time house rules
No bad words
No yelling or whining

No stomping feet
No raising hand with a closed fist
No back talk
No fighting or rough housing
Say please, thank you, and you're welcome
Do extra reading before 8:00 p.m.
No rewards if you are in a consequence
No points are allowed to be spent during a consequence
Go to bed when Mom or Dad tells you
Follow unwritten rules

Rewards

10 points = 10 extra computer time
15 points = 20 extra computer and iPad time
20 points = 30 extra computer, iPad, and TV time

Consequences for Breaking Rules

1 breath (If a rule is broken, even if it is not listed here, you say "breath." Children stop and you slide into neutral.)
Lose screen time (iPad) for 15 minutes
Lose screen time (iPad and computer) for 15 minutes
Lose screen time (iPad, computer, and TV) for 15 minutes
Lose screen time (iPad, computer, and TV) for a day

Sign here: _____

These parents went a step further, and while regulating their children, they were building citizens of their home. They implemented a chore chart as well as a schedule. We have left blank spaces so you may individualize your own chart. Please note that the children knew what the expectations were for "preparing for bed" and "make sure your room is neat and tidy" before they implemented the chart. Those specifics were reviewed at a family meeting. Here are their charts:

MORE ON RULE BREAKING

You may also add new rules when something arises at home that warrants a rule. State: "I have witnessed a new problem. Has anyone else seen the problem?" Then introduce and discuss your new rule. Behavioral consequences should not be given if a child does not know the rule, but you can add a new rule after a rule was broken unknowingly. If a rule is broken and you really believe the child had no idea that he or she did something wrong, talk about it. This happens most often with unwritten rules. The child may admit that he or she didn't know the rule. Be a good listener and allow your child to speak. Remain quiet, make eye contact, and evaluate the situation in your head (you will want to think about what needs to happen next, or cause and effect). Be neutral. You may choose to give a behavioral consequence next time for a poor decision made, but the child should be commended for not lying. Adults or children can add to the rule chart anytime at a family meeting. This keeps the "randomness" out of making rules. Don't be surprised if you need more paper, not because it is "so bad," but because children like boundaries and security. Rules produce boundaries, and children and adults live happily within boundaries. We all know that when there are no laws, or rules, people get unruly, violent, angry, and out of control, both in mind and body.

In addition, you may have a special area for the child to sit during a consequence. When you default to your word, your child may choose to plop on the couch and that is fine too. Don't pay attention to the plopping down of your child's body. Even if the "plop on the couch" bothers you, ignore it. Addressing it would be adding a negative to the situation. We also suggest you avoid a struggle to get the child to "the place" to do the so-called consequence. We do not suggest you "put" the child in time-out, as that leads nowhere fast. The child will do it him- or herself and will find a place to take the "consequence." You will begin to find yourself reviewing the rules less, and subsequently there will be fewer issues erupting at home.

Teach the rules when they are not being broken.

Table 6.1: Example of a Chart for House Rules

Chores	Mon	Tues	Wed	Thur	Fri	Sat	Sun
Daily							
Make the bed							
Put dirty clothes in the hamper							
Put all toys and books away							
Make sure room is neat and tidy							
Think positive thoughts for the day							
Help in the kitchen (i.e., set the table, get food, put dishes in the dishwasher)							
Other assigned chores							
Sunday							
Complete daily chores							
Help in the kitchen with dinner							
Work on homework							
Prepare for bedtime							
Monday							
Complete daily chores							
Help in the kitchen with dinner							

Table 6.1: Continued

Chores	Mon	Tues	Wed	Thur	Fri	Sat	Sun
Work on homework							
Prepare for bedtime							
Tuesday							
Complete daily chores							
Help in the kitchen with dinner							
Work on homework							
Prepare for bedtime							
Wednesday							
Complete daily chores							
Help in the kitchen with dinner							
Work on homework							
Prepare for bedtime							
Thursday							
Complete daily chores							
Help in the kitchen with dinner							
Work on homework							
Prepare for bedtime							

(Continued)

Table 6.1: Continued

Chores	Mon	Tues	Wed	Thur	Fri	Sat	Sun
Friday							
Complete daily chores							
Help in the kitchen with dinner							
Work on homework							
Prepare for bedtime							
Saturday							
Complete daily chores							
Help in the kitchen with dinner							
Work on homework							
Prepare for bedtime							

MELTDOWNS

When your child has a temper tantrum or meltdown, do three things. First, scan the situation and make sure your child is safe. Next, use your default word. Then, when your child takes a breath (this is natural) and stops the behavior, begin to sight that he or she is controlling him- or herself and you can see he or she is breathing and calming down. Stay calm and give little attention to the meltdown. Address the moment of breath and then sight what has changed for the better. This is the feedback we highly encourage, and it is imperative to the behavior change.

WHAT IS FEEDBACK

Feedback is a response or reaction to your child's behavior, action, task, or performance (discussed in chapter 8). It may be verbal, written, or gestural. During the learning process, the purpose of feedback is to improve a child's behavior, definitely not put a damper on it. When it's given immediately after a positive behavior, the child links the action to the feedback and is inclined to repeat the positive behavior to gain more feedback. It's a victorious cycle (opposite of vicious). Remember: Give no *immediate* feedback for a negative behavior, just your "word" and a slide into neutral. The ultimate goal of feedback is to provide children with information that helps them continue positive behaviors and extinguish negative ones.

The use of negative body language, sarcasm, eye rolling, and huffing and puffing over behavior is *not at all acceptable*. Children will always remember how you made them feel, and you want to build a positive rapport that is lifelong.

When you tell your child that he or she is important, and matters to you, you are supplying your child with positive attention. Provide words of love and affection, so your child feels valued and loved. When you concentrate on positive attention before the negative happens, you teach the rules in a simplistic, nontraditional way. You would not say, "Oh, you broke rule number eight, you better go sit in the time-out chair." Note only the positive, thereby teaching your child to strive to be positive in behavioral, cognitive, and social domains.

THE POINT CREDIT SYSTEM

It's important to understand that when parents use the credit system, they are working from an external point of view. That means the parent uses additional outside support to gain a positive behavior response or the support is given when the parent "creates" a positive behavior response in the midst of a happening or after the child performs a positive behavior response. This is a short-term goal, which builds instant success. It creates a sense of self-worth and importance in the child, as well as a sense of purpose in the family unit. It is literally conditioning. It is common for children to test, but you should remain cool, calm, and collected. The negative will be undermined by your neutrality, and you will be able to use your "breathe word" to pull your child back toward receiving a credit.

Do *not* give credits during meltdowns, overreactive behaviors such as body language "fits," tantrums, the breaking of rules, and the like. Once the "breathe word" is spoken and your child changes behavior, quickly find something positive to say about your child or his or her action and give credit. There is always something positive to find about any child. Your immediate goal is to show a vast comparison between positive and negative behaviors and show how positive attention is given to positive actions and neutrality is given to negative ones.

We highly encourage the credit system be short and sweet and that parents wean their children from it as soon as possible, as we do not want it to backfire. A child can begin refusing to do a chore or task while holding the parent for ransom for the reward. Don't allow it to get to this point. Reevaluate your methods; find where you may be slipping and change it. It is all a learning process. Start each moment anew. Most likely you are not using your words sufficiently, or you may not be "sighting" enough of what you see, and the child has become dependent on the points and credits. Increase your positive words and cut back a bit for a time on giving credits. This will help correct any negative situations one step at a time, without "withdrawals" from the credit system.

RECAP

In the beginning, tickets flow freely and rewards (from your behavior chart) are the goal for tickets cashed. As you move forward and feel more comfortable with the program, you can begin to lessen the number of tickets given, replace them with more verbal language, affection, kudos, and nonmaterialistic rewards for jobs well done. We have seen many children forget about tickets and become enthralled in all the other positive rewards the parent doles out.

In addition to credits, you will continue to reward your child through positive language, attitude, household climate, breathing exercises, and meditation times. The reward begins to become internalized within the child. The satisfaction and feeling of success will begin to take over, and your child's self-esteem will rise. Your child will become happy with him- or herself and the positive sightings from those who support and care for him or her. You will "feel" the time is right to start lessening the number of tickets you give each day.

Ultimately, the goal is for your child to internalize that feeling of accomplishment and success and be "self-rewarded." It is a process by which you move forward each and every time you feel good about a success or job well done. You add to your social, emotional, and cognitive well-being, as well as actualize or become mindful of your limitations, as you move through life. When you do one thing that makes you proud, without being externally rewarded, and you feel a sense of positive self-worth, you are well on your way to doing it again and again.

TICKETS EARNED ARE KEPT AND NEVER REMOVED AS PUNISHMENT FOR NEGATIVE BEHAVIORS

We have seen the removal of credits create mistrust, stress, stealing, and greed. We do not advise this type of intervention in our program, Negative behavior charts reflect punitive connotations, such as going down a rung on a ladder, moving a space backward on the line, or erasing a check mark. There are apps and technical programs for phones and computers that help parents track "good and bad behaviors," and they also keep track of points given and points taken away from children. The negativity of these apps represents a practice long overdue for retirement. Guiding and supporting engagement, persistence, and positive interactions and lots of feedback help promote growth and success in interrelationships.

BUYING WITH CREDIT

Credit spending is not bargaining. Your child should not say, "If I do this, what do I get?" Nor should your child spend credits during a consequence or have entire control over rewards. You do not give rewards to stop negative behavior; they should be consistent with the rule chart. No changes should be made or negotiations given unless the family decides to make changes once goals are met. The reward should be within reason and one that the parent can still control. Here are some examples for younger and older children:

- Getting extra computer time, game time, or TV time
- Enjoying a small cupcake or small amount of candy, ice cream, fruit, fruit snacks, pretzels, low-salt chips, or other foods
- Taking a trip to a dollar store to buy one or two items
- Watching a movie at home or out
- Taking a bike ride with friends or a trusting adult
- Doing a cooking project, making homemade modeling clay or slime, or doing another arts and crafts project
- Having a sleepover
- Getting a favorite fast food or dinner choice
- Doing a science experiment
- Having a pizza night
- Making a fort
- Temporary tattoos
- Skipping a chore for a day
- Staying up fifteen to minutes extra at night
- Sleeping in on a Saturday or Sunday

Finally, while you teach rules when they are not broken, we would also suggest you have family meetings to discuss and solve real-life problems. The following are scenarios from families we have worked with and others from our experiences with children as professionals.

> *Walking before solving a problem improves your creativity by an average of 60 percent.*

Chart 6.4: Problem-Solving Scenarios

For each scenerio, think: "What do I do and/or what do I say to solve the problem?"

- Your sibling borrowed something from you and has not returned it.
- You asked your parents if a friend could sleepover on the weekend. They said no.
- You shared your lunch with someone who did not have lunch and then he or she bought ice cream with the money you loaned them.

- You are taking a test and the person at the desk next to you keeps looking at your paper.
- You are getting ready to line up after lunch and someone cuts the line in front of you.
- You are sitting at your desk and your neighbor at the desk next to you is throwing paper balls at you when the teacher is not looking.
- Lots of your friends are playing kickball, but when you ask to join a team they say no.
- There is no room for you on the swings and no one is getting off.
- You get on the bus and go to your assigned seat, but it is taken by someone else.
- You forgot your homework and it was due today.
- You overslept for dance class. Mom is rushing and telling you to hurry up, as you are already late. When you get there, the dance teacher is already teaching all the students.
- You are shopping with holiday money and, after making a purchase, you can't find your wallet.

Children understand that not everyone has the same opinion. Two children in the same family may have different answers to the above scenarios. But there are appropriate and inappropriate answers, and safe and unsafe procedures. It's the parents "responsibility" to make sure they facilitate open, honest, and trusting communication with their child. Parents teach values, respect of others, and their opinions in exercises like discussing these scenarios. No judgments should be passed, and there should be no put downs or negative connotations, but there should be a great deal of discussion and problem-solving.

A parent may choose this as a time to say, "Remember this week when you had a problem with your chores? Let's take the time to think about how to solve that issue, so it does not become commonplace." There are times when you can wait on a behavior like missing chores to discuss at a later time, but remember feedback is most important and understood when it is given at of calm, controlled intervals. Seize the opportunity to commend your child for answering honestly and explaining how he or she would handle the problem and the solution. Be reminded of rules, boundaries, and limitations, as you proceed in this activity.

SUMMARY

This chapter offered a plethora of information in which we covered rule making and regulatory skills. A good behavior management program includes your "word" of choice to begin the process of changing behavior for the betterment of all involved. We discussed how you may use a the image of a balanced scale and your verbal sighting to create a positive influence, away from the negativity that is not working and never will work in changing your child's behavior long-term. We wrote about our own experiences with real-life parents and children who made changes and are productive people to this day. The credit system is something you may decide to use to help yourself get started and see quick results, but it is also something that should not be used long-term and should be weaned from over a few weeks to a few months. Families make the rules, and family time is stressed as a healthy component of our program. Family time scenarios were supplied in this chapter to begin the process of regular scheduled meetings to solve problems within the family. Feedback is important to support your child now and in their future. We supplied you with sample rule charts and chore charts and discussed meltdowns, anger, and temper tantrums and how you default to our program while remaining consistent and neutral in your dealings of behaviors.

Chapter Seven

Setting the Stage for R #4 Regulation

> Emotional self-control—delaying gratification and stifling impulsiveness—underlies accomplishment of every sort.
>
> —Daniel Goleman

As children grow, it is appropriate for them to learn regulation of mind and body and to work toward goals. This is a lifelong task that even some adults have to work to master. The earlier we introduce this concept in the home, and in the school curriculum, and the more self-control and self-regulation strategies children know and use, the easier it becomes for them to accomplish their academic and social goals. Self-regulation results in improved behavior. When behavior improves, so should decision making.

Attention is an important part of self-regulation. Attention helps us focus on goals and control our emotions. Regulation takes years to attain. Toddlers are developing mental skills that support self-regulation, while elementary school–aged children have the basic ability to focus attention for longer periods of time, describe and discuss emotions, and resist doing inappropriate things as part of their social, emotional, and cognitive development. The part of the brain that helps us to self-regulate is the prefrontal cortex. It doesn't fully mature until early adulthood. Even as adults many people struggle to self-regulate at different times.

WHAT IS THE DEFINITION OF SELF-CONTROL AND SELF-REGULATION?

The Table below will clear up any misconceptions between the terms *self-control* and *self-regulation*, as they are similar and used interchangeably, but in essence they are different.

Table 7.1: *Comparison of Self-Regulation vs. Self-Control*

Self-Regulation	Self-Control
Self-regulation makes self-control possible by reducing the frequency and intensity of strong impulses, managing stress-load, and moving through recovery. Self-regulation focuses on the "thinking brain," or the executive function area of the brain or the pre-frontal area.	Self-control is about inhibiting strong impulses. It involves the center of the brain, or the hippocampus or limbic area.
Self-regulation is planning and modulating your action to avoid problems. In other words, "planning before the fact." It is important to remember that self-regulation strategies must be taught, and it is better to start at a young age.	When thinking about self, think that it is a mental activity. It is like stepping on the brake to stop a car. If you don't step on the brake early enough, you must plan next time to do it earlier. Act early or plan later.
Self-regulation involves actions using the executive "learning brain."	Self-control involves reactions and occurs in the "survival brain" (cerebellum or lower brain), which is in the center of the brain.
Self-regulation occurs in the prefrontal cortex—the home of our rational, reflective self.	Think of self-control in terms of "cognitive competencies," i.e., things like reappraisal, self-distraction, self-soothing, or weighting the consequences of an action. When a reaction to an event occurs in the limbic area, the brain goes into survival mode.
Actions are suppressed in the PFC area when the brain is in "survival mode," since the brain is concerned about survival, as it is the most important task.	"Self-control" is not likened to deciding to speed, but more like slowing down to prevent an accident. It's really a case of averting an accident and stepping on the brake before it is too late.

Table 7.1:   Continued

Self-Regulation	Self-Control
Children are only able to develop and use their cognitive ability if their arousal has been reduced by practicing self-regulation. We accomplish this by identifying and reducing stressors when they are hyper-aroused and knowing what self-regulation strategies to use before it is too late.	Children get stimulated and aroused (this occurs in the limbic area, or mid-brain), which shuts down their thinking. When the limbic system is aroused, one of three things occurs: fight, flight, or fear.
Self-regulation speaks to the importance of reframing behavior, distinguishing between misbehavior and stress behavior. For that to be possible, we should recognize the signs of stress behavior.	Parenting skills focuses on teaching children about the consequences of their actions and how to recall the lessons when needed to develop self-control.
The vital importance of self-regulation also tells us that we often talk (or worse) when we should be listening—with our eyes as much as our ears.	What neuroscience suggests is that "kids" learn less from lectures, and more from doing tasks or applying what they have learned.
Self-regulation reduces arousal and reaction to stimuli to bring back those reflective capacities.	Self-control reduces self-regulation, as it trumps self-regulation.

> *The difference between self-regulation and self-control lies deep within the brain.*

A BIT OF BRAIN RESEARCH

If you had the ability to look inside the brain of a child who is highly aroused, you would see a limbic system lit up in bright shades of red. The limbic system, which is the source of strong emotions and impulses, is in control and overrides other parts of the brain. Therefore we say "all learning is emotional." When we calm down and feel the situation is safe, good decision making, and appropriate behaviors happen. The brain is always in survival mode, as survival is a strong instinct. The task is to move from survival mode (where the limbic system dictates actions) to learning mode (where the pre-frontal area makes decisions). As stated earlier, the shift from "survival brain" to "learning brain" is critical for learning, self-control, self-regulation, and appropriate behavior choices

When people think of self-control, they think trying to force the brain to ignore or drown out negative emotions. A simple way to do this is with breathing strategies, such as taking a deep breath and counting to ten. Now, it is apparent why we linked mediation, breathing, and reflection to our own program. It is the most natural way to control behaviors.

More advanced methods of self-control would include things like finding ways to distract ourselves or taking a moment to consider the consequences of what we are doing. This requires a lot of executive function (prefrontal cortex) and self-regulatory skills, and this takes time to master.

In order to self-regulate, we have to first identify the stressors that cause negative emotions and work to reduce or eliminate them. Parents should encourage the identification process and help their child learn to regulate by recognizing stressors or triggers and then provide the strategies and techniques to learn to cope effectively.

IMPORTANT BRAIN STEPS FOR SELF-REGULATION

The *first step* in the self-regulation process is called *foreknowledge*. Actually, foreknowledge is the first step in any process of developing an action plan and knowing what needs to be done. Foreknowledge enables a child to know what she will need to become regulated.

As part of the home climate, the parent will introduce strategies such as breathing, imagery, and reflection as the foundation for the self-regulation process. By doing so, the parent is creating an atmosphere within the household, so regulation can fall into place. With an early introduction to these strategies, the child will carry them throughout her life and well into adulthood.

You may have seen someone use the breathing technique to control her emotions during a time of crisis.

Self-talk is an essential component during self-regulation. It encourages instant self-reflection. It requires independent thinking, breathing, and, finally, regulation by the child. Self-talk is highly encouraged in order for the child to work toward the process of regulation.

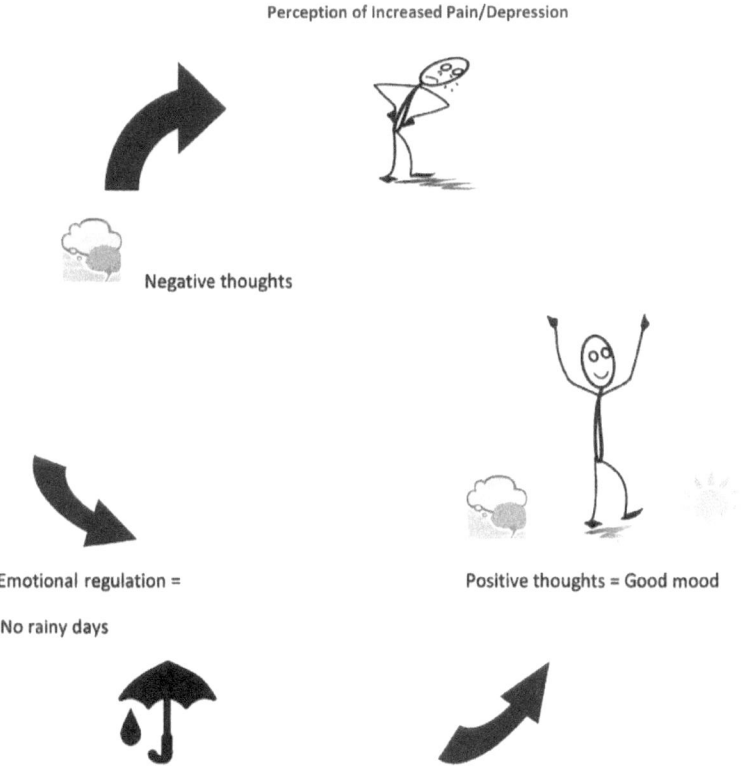

Figure 7.1:   Comparison of Self-Regulation vs. Self Control.

A SCENARIO

Two siblings are fighting over the same truck. One "wins" the truck and the other has an "angry moment."

Angry Child: I want that truck!
The child *does not* immediately use the self-regulation strategy, as he is *in a moment of fight or flight (emotional response)* and does not regulate well at his young age. He still needs guidance to regulate. The older child, who has learned more about self-regulation and has practiced it more, has some self-regulation skills, so stopping the action is easier for him. In addition, the children's parent needs to put an emphasis on self-regulation activities like breathing, tapping, role modeling, and so

on for the younger child, as well as reinforcing those same strategies in the older child.

Parent: BREATHE.
There is little time taken for the consequence. The angry child takes her PAUSE BREATH very well, and the parent is able to begin her sightings.
Both children stop the behavior and sit still until …

Parent: "I see that your loud voice and red face are disappearing now." The parent is just noticing "for" the child what he should be feeling and hearing in himself, which is that the temperature in his face is lowering and his voice is deescalating. (You have practiced this in an earlier chapter and have been implementing it in real time with your child). The parent's sightings alert the child that he is regulating well, and the so-called "breathe" moment is over. Begin problem solving when all is calm.

Parent: "What can you do to help yourself feel better right now?"
The parent does not address the problem, as it is the *problem* that escalated the unregulated behavior. She is waiting for the calm moment when the angry child is in better control. She does not want to miss the opportunity, so she is using her "stick-to-it-ness" and watching intently. The parent begins to guide the child into reflection by reminding him of the strategies she has taught him to use when he feels angry. The parent is also telling the child that she trusts him to gain control and/or that she will help him. The child may begin to recognize his internal feelings.

Note: The parent may *not* be able to observe a calm face. If the child is still demanding and angry, she should continue the BREATHE strategy. Keep an eye out for physical negative behaviors, as little ones can resort to hitting. (This is because they do not have regulation, and often it is also because they cannot express their feelings.) At some point, and as timely as possible, the parent will begin to interject the change of behavior from red, angry face to calming down face as described below.

If hitting begins, the important thing is to keep the other child safe. In this scenario the parent may have to walk between the two children and escort the other child away from the hitter. The parent needs to stay neutral and just walk away with the child in a calm manner. As she finds an out-of-the-way area for the child, she will turn and calmly say "Breathe" to the hitter, and then begin to sight that the hitter is controlling his temper and his hands are not hitting anymore. Do you remember the balance scale? The more positive you give, the less these actions occur, but until you tip the scale toward the positive side, you will need to pour on the positive sightings and keep the safety factor in check. When it is time to speak and discuss, the parent may want to ask, "What were you thinking just before you hit your brother?" This will help the child focus on his feelings and lead to the ability to "feel" what is happening just before lashing out and potentially controlling the hitting hands.

Parent: "I see you are breathing normally now. You did a great job counting. I could hear you count from one to ten in a controlled way. Great self-talk (parent is sighting what is happening). I see your head is up and that you are thinking about how to control your body. Nice job. ("Nice job" is not empty praise, as it comes with sightings). You are making good changes. You have your normal face and you are using an inside voice."

The parent has built a foundation of success. She is helping her child to self-regulate, even though she may not be seeing it happen "exactly" as one would expect or desire. This is OK, as the parent continues the practice and helps the desired behavior emerge in the near future.

Child: Mumbling under breath; repeating "breathe" to himself (self-talk). The child is breathing in through his nose and out though his mouth. He is calm, due to the breathing mechanism and the neurological system. This is why "breathing" is a natural word choice, as it is an involuntary action. There is always a success with it.

Child: Breathes and counts in a low voice and sits down on the floor.

Parent: Very aware, but not displaying an overreaction.

Child: Stands up and comes over to the parent and says "I don't want to play with my brother."

Parent: "I hear what you are saying, and I saw how upset you were a moment ago. How do we solve your problem? Do you have any ideas?"

Parent and child discuss the problem and solution together. Until the child showed an attempt at regulating his behavior, the parent remained aware, neutral, but "out of the problem." She kept her eyes on the child to make sure he was safe and secure, and she added very few words, just enough to prime the child to begin the independent action of regulation. When the child was feeling less stressed, the child came over to the parent who was waiting for him. She did not give any negative feedback to the child, like "Snap out of it." or "You started it with your brother." The parent used open-ended questioning to help gain solutions. In this case the child was not ready to figure it out for himself, so the parent addressed it by prompting him to refer to a past practice, which is the use of a timer.

Parent: "Do you remember when we used a timer (in the problematic past] last time this happened? Do you remember how it helped you and your brother take turns sharing?"

Parent continues to work through the problem until both siblings are using the timer and cooperating with each other. Parent sights the cooperation and sharing between the brothers.

Another scenario that may have occurred is that the child regulated and then, instead of coming to the parent, would have addressed his brother with the truck. The child may suggest that they share, based on the use of a timer for this purpose. This is a solution that has been discussed and practiced in the household. In this case, the parent would keep a keen eye on the articulation between the brothers and the body language of both children, while watching the problem solve itself. The parent would only intervene if help were needed (as in the note above), or if there were an escalation during the sharing. The parent will want to give "real" praise by stating that she is witnessing cooperation, problem-solving, and more. Using words like "good job" is fine to add to sightings, as well as "thank you," as long as it comes with sightings that make it sincere and with no empty praise. Here is an example: "Thank you for solving your own problems by using our family timer. I am very proud of you."

If the child just gives up and retreats, as some children may do, the parent intervenes and role models the skills of sharing and cooperation. Self-control will be apparent, but the lack of "energy" given to problem-solving is an issue that needs to be addressed, so that the child learns how to solve conflicts. This scenario took time, but it is time well spent now, so that less time is spent later.

The *second step* is to work on a home environment that promotes self-regulation. The self-regulated environment is purposeful and meaningful and encourages the use mediation, reflection, breathing strategies, self-talk, sightings, and "stickability" (or "stick-to-it-ness") by all members of the household. It includes character education traits and allows the child to think for herself with guidance from the parent. The parent creates rules and boundaries and works the Student Empowerment Program© correctly.

The *third step* is for the adult members of the home to monitor their progress when using our program. You will also want to monitor the children's progress and the children should monitor their own progress as well. Rule charts may need to be changed, consequences faded and replaced by self-directed pseudo consequences, and a credit system initiated and then weaned. In addition, sightings should become "normal" and less stilted in speech. The atmosphere is beginning to change toward a positive one. Making time for these strategies, as part of daily living builds success.

SUMMARY

In this chapter, we clarified the difference between self-control and self-regulation. We discussed the brain's function as it relates to regulation. The brain's function is our survival. If there is a threatening situation, we flee the situation and go to a safe place. Therefore, it is important that we create a safe environment for children to learn and grow. Once we have a safe environment, we can develop self-regulation skills to handle situations in an effective and efficient way. This process involves developing self-regulation skills, which is a three-step process and must be used and practiced, so they become second nature. We provided an example of a parent helping her children learn to self-regulate, and we discussed her "stick-to-it-ness" or "stickabilty." We suggested that parents don't give in or give up, just start again.

Chapter Eight

Setting the Stage for R #5 Rubrics

Too often we give children answers to remember, rather than problems to solve."

—Roger Lewin

A rubric is an assessment tool. It provides a continuous and consistent manner in which a child can assess his or her progress based on standards, and it keeps all interpretations fair and equal. It is a common tool used in schools, and this tool can be used at home. This is your choice. We suggest you use a rubric once you have positive results from the Student Empowerment Program©, and you have changed behavior through goal setting.

Please note your rubric does not have to be in graph form. Many people use a verbal rubric by asking how the child did on the task.

The Student Empowerment Program© is an ongoing program, and new goals are always implemented. Once your child understands that you are committed to a new form of behavior management, and she begins to show signs of improvement, you may consider a rubric to increase your child's thinking power, independence, and regulation.

Beginning in early childhood, children can compare two objects or even ideas. They use their executive function to plan, set goals, and evaluate outcomes. The youngest child can evaluate if she did or did not put away toys correctly, and the older child can decide if she loaded and unloaded the dishwasher correctly.

THE EARLY CHILDHOOD BRAIN ON RUBRICS

The early childhood brain is complex, and children are learning at rapid rates in school and at home. The goal is for parents to help their children strive toward self-regulation and success, and for their children to be able change failures into learning experiences. A rubric assists the child in the process of becoming an intelligent citizen and lifelong learner. By instilling a sense of success in the learner, the parent also develops motivation in the child.

A rubric is an integral part of The Student Empowerment Program© because it promotes success by allowing the child to take charge of learning and regulation. The child determines what needs to be done to advance to the next level. It also allows the child to become an independent learner and seek resources needed to complete the goal with feedback from the parent.

You will begin to teach your child how to use her thoughts and feedback by evaluating her work. In other words, you will teach your child to be reflective of her performance. Your child's performance may be social, cognitive, emotional, and/or academic. You may want to use only one rubric in the home, and it is your choice which one. You may choose to use only verbal feedback and questioning. We will provide you with examples that will help you choose the right one for your child and household. You certainly do not want to become school-like, using rubrics for everything in your home, but you may want to try one to take your child to another level of learning.

Parents have standards at home, just as teachers have standards in school. Rubrics in school are used throughout the curriculum, and we suggest you work with your child's teacher to secure a good home/school relationship, which includes the use of rubrics in school and at home. School standards are behavioral, academic, and social. Home standards are behavioral, academic, and social too! By working with your child's teacher, you can target many of the same goals. This home/school connection is an imperative one.

In essence, when you wrote your family rules you wrote your standards, similar to the ones teachers write with students in school, so why not implement a system of checks and balances? A system that when implemented helps your child write a rule and then check her progress toward a goal. A child must have some regulatory skills for this to happen, and that is why we suggest you use it after you begin to see your child respond well to our program.

WRITTEN RUBRICS AND VERBAL RUBRICS

When you ask your child to set the kitchen table for dinner, you have standards: one fork, one knife, one spoon, one plate, one napkin, and one glass for each member of the family. What if your child only set four out of five of the place settings, or missed all of the forks when setting the table? You might tell her to put another setting out or add forks. This is a direct answer in your "old life," but in your new thought process, you would do a verbal analysis. You might say, "So how did you do with the table setting? Does everyone have one fork, one knife, and so on? Tell me about the number of people and the number of settings you have prepared."

Let's look at this from another point of view. The original quote at the top of this chapter stated, "We give children answers to remember, rather than problems to solve." Often this is true, because we want to get moving, get out of the house, get to an appointment on time, or just make things easier in general, and we tell the child what to do just to get it done. Teachers make this mistake too. When a child says, "I don't know what to do," the teacher directs her again by stating the same direction over or maybe changing the wording a bit, but the teacher is still telling the child what she expects and almost how to do it. Then, the teacher may question the child's listening skills to check for understanding. This works quite well with the average child, but some children will be "lost in the woods."

It would be better for the teacher to ask, "What part of the direction did you need help with? What *do* you understand?" Then the teacher can begin the reflection process and facilitate the child to complete the process by herself. This also is a self-esteem builder. A parent can do the same at home. Use the same format next time your child does something that is incomplete, such as putting away homework or putting away her coat, shoes, and book bag. You can say, "You did so well putting your coat in the closet. What's next?"

Many children do hear the direction clearly, but may not be motivated, may lack self-confidence, or may not be a self-starter and so they don't act on the direction. They may have missed one part of the direction and just need some help with it. This is why we encourage parents to use the questioning and reflective processes.

We know through our program that the chapter on reflection helped you make your child an independent and reflective thinker and one who is headed toward better regulatory skills. In the case of the table-setting example (a written rubric example), you will apply that same concept. This time, do not give an answer to the table-setting chore, but direct your child in an informal way to do a self-check or rubric.

With an older child you may want to say, "Double-check your task/work, and let me know how you did." The older child understands, from years of practice, how to set a table and can recall from memory the sequence of the task. This child will probably report back to the parent that she is fixing one mistake, or maybe she will just fix the mistake and say, "All done, Mom." In the case of a younger child, you may post this picture as an expectation for a table setting. As the parent you introduce the sequence of events involved in setting the table. You discuss the fork, spoon, knife, plate, napkin, and glass. You model for the child how a table is set, and you practice it. You lead by modeling.

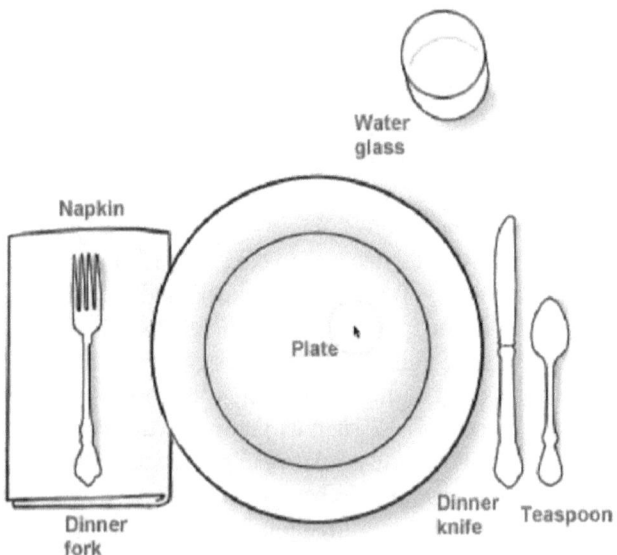

Chart 8.1: Rubric for Setting the Table.

Setting the Stage for R #5 Rubrics 91

This is done so many times in your child's life, and it is important that you understand the importance of building a foundation for your child by helping her become an independent thinker. This is not to say you will never help your child, but it is important to encourage her to think first and ask for help second.

The final step is allowing your child to do it alone. This time, the younger child will use the picture example of a table setting to make sure that each of the family members has all parts of the setting. The number 6 is an imperative number, as it is the self-check for which you are looking. Your child may count like this: Person 1, 2, and 3 each have 1, 2, 3 spoons, they each have 1, 2, 3 forks, they each have 1, 2, 3 knives, and so on and so forth. This self-evaluation of her table setting is now a verbal rubric done reflectively by the child, based on the experience of the model rubric.

Here is a formal use of a rubric at home and one we find is fun, as well as helpful, for children. Using the same example of a table setting, you and your child can discuss verbally or use a model of a rubric that looks like this:

I am ready to set the table for ____people (#?)	Almost	Got it done.	Hmmm... How did I do?
Each setting has a 1. Fork 2. Knife 3. Spoon 4. Plate 5. Napkin 6. Glass	I missed some and I fixed it.	Got it done.	Hmmm... How did I do?

Chart 8.2:   Rubric For "How Did I Do?"

This rubric allows your child to follow a model. It is not much different than reading a map. Once you learn the steps, you navigate your way through a rubric until you reach your destination or goal. The child begins by viewing the first box, where she is directed to be ready to start and list the number of people for whom she is setting the table. Next, the child circles that box to show she has started. A check or a slash line or any pencil mark is fine, as long as the child knows to complete it. Next, she moves on to the second box, which names the six items that must be at each place setting. Once the child has completed that task, she can check off "got it done" and move on to the reflection piece called "How Did I Do?" While she is cognizant of the six items, she may realize he or she forgot one and can circle "I missed one and I fixed it." This is a board game for the child, and it is very well received and fun. Finally, after all is done, the child reflects and hopefully announces she has completed the goal.

As a parent you will want to tell your child that you were watching and she was working so hard and was really conscientious of her job. You may say that she did a great job because everyone has all the parts to the place setting necessary to eat tonight. Remember "great job" can be vague, so you may want to continue to name the actions associated with the great job, depending upon how much external support your child needs. You are basing your kudos on internalization of a job well done vs. external needs for support. This will be a big hit with your child. If at any time you see your child struggling with the rubric, watch, allow for some time for thought, and then ask her if there is a part for which she would like some help. Try very hard not to give away the answer, but encourage reflection, revisiting and trying again.

Remember, "Practice makes perfect and perfect practice makes practice perfect." This is a quote Dr. Barbiere used when he coached his son's teams in sports many years ago. It also applies to the basic premise of rubrics. Students will feel empowered when they use their rubric at home, and they view it as a self-challenge.

A rubric provides the opportunity to research for step-by-step instructions too. For instance, if your teen wants to learn how to do something, such as change the oil in a car, she might go to a website and follow along with the step-by-step process. The step-by-step visual and oral process displayed on the computer is a rubric in the most disguised form. Your teen can watch and complete the steps one by one and check to see if she did it correctly. At the end of the video, she checks again to make sure she did it all correctly and starts the car. Success! The car starts and the oil is dispersed.

For a younger child, seeing a model of how to write her name or using capital letters and punctuation marks helps build successes during homework time. Always remember to provide feedback and sightings when your child is working on her accomplishment.

> *The hypothalamus gets the adrenaline flowing during a test.*

Chart for Name Writing (Systematic)

Write your first, middle and last name on the lines. Use the model to help you form the letter correctly.

        John Jay Doe

Chart 8.3:   Chart for Name Writing.

Name: _____

Directions: Write a short story with 2-4 sentences.

Color in the bubble if you did it.

Question yourself; what bubbles are not colored in?

Draw a picture to go with your story.

	<ul><li>USE CAPITALS</li><li>Use finger space between words.</li><li>End with a period ●</li><li>Reread your ☉☉ sentences.</li></ul>

Chart 8.4: Simple Rubric for Capitals and Punctuation (systematic).

Table 8.1: Rubric for Reading (Systematic)

	Beginning	Progressing	Developed
Books	I read one chapter today.	I read two chapters today.	I read three chapters today.
Student Reflection	I did what was assigned.	I did an extra chapter of reading today.	1 did two extra chapters today.

A Creative Rubric for any use (systematic but thinking not as stringent --outside the box)

	✔ Comments	✔ ✔ Comments	✔ ✔ ✔ Comments	✔ ✔ ✔ ✔ Comments
Brainstorming and daydreaming				
Thinking and Inquiry and possible solutions				
Creativity and eliminate negativity in problem solving				

Chart 8.5: Rubric for Reading (Systematic).

SUMMARY

In this chapter, we discussed rubrics. A rubric is an assessment tool that provides a continuous and consistent manner in which a child can assess her progress based on standards and keeps all interpretations fair and equal. Please remember that your rubric does not have to be in graph form, as many people use a verbal rubric.

The Student Empowerment Program© is a dynamic program, and new goals are always implemented. Once your child understands that you have committed to a new form of behavior management, and she begins to show signs of changing, then you can use a rubric to increase your child's thinking power, independence and self-regulation.

Chapter Nine

Setting the Stage for the Finale

The most courageous act is still to think for yourself. Aloud.

—Coco Chanel

In the previous chapters we addressed the Student Empowerment Program© and the 5 Rs©: *responsibility, reflection, rules, regulation, and rubrics*. Throughout this book you've read about techniques and strategies and learned about the brain and its function. This chapter will review this process and act as a quick reference guide, as you implement the Student Empowerment Program© in your home.

You have taken the first step toward making positive behavioral changes by purchasing this book. Throughout the book we have provided a step-by-step process for you to follow. The Student Empowerment Program© explains how to take measures to create a series of consistent changes that will result in positive outcomes for you and your child, family, and household. Raising a child who is responsible in our ever-changing world is your greater goal, and we will help you set the stage for the foundation you need to begin that process.

Responsibility, or the first R, is your determination and commitment to read and implement the strategies and techniques in this book. Responsibility is the understanding that you can create a change in yourself and in the world around you. You will be building success in your child by facilitating her to become an independent person who is in charge of her own learning. You will teach your child to communicate, collaborate, think critically and creatively, and learn responsibility and good citizenship skills. Teaching your child to be accountable for his or her actions, and how to problem solve with and without interventions, are momentous feats for you to conquer. We trust that you can do it! Use your "stickabilty,"and if you make a mistake, start over. There is no need to wait, as each moment is a new beginning and an opportunity to start anew.

Take a moment to reflect about you, your child, your family, and the responsibility each person has in the household and the responsibility you have to each other. Revisit the questions in Chapter Four and discover why you need to make changes by isolating these thoughts. Think to yourself, *I can conquer the ones that are interfering with the ones that make me smile.* This is highly responsible, and we trust that you have come to realize you are not alone in these feelings. In our years as professionals, we have addressed many parents who start out the same as you and end up learning to parent with their eyes wide open. You are going to repair what needs to be fixed, and you will stop asking others to "fix my child," because you will have the toolbox full of the 5Rs© to build success and self-regulation within your own family. The onus of learning and maturing will be on your child with you as the facilitator.

Reflection, or the second R is a fun one and one that really helps your child with self-regulation. In Chapter Five we discovered that changes take place in the prefrontal cortex of the brain and executive function is necessary for regulation. We also know that during times of stress, our prefrontal cortex responds with what researchers call the "fight or flight" response. We know that certain parts of the brain are active when we are in fight or flight mode, and we can react by either fighting or fleeing during stress. That means that when there is a situation that is negative, we either react to it or we avoid it.

Knowing this bit of brain information is important, because reflection plays a huge part in controlling oneself during times of stress. For a child, stress can exhibit itself in several ways including stomachaches, headaches, meltdowns, temper tantrums, augments, nervous habits, depression, avoidance, or lashing out verbally or physically. Many parents have sought the help of professionals in response to childhood stress, and only you know what is best for your child. We simply encourage you to use reflection as a mindfulness tool. We are not here to diagnose, as we leave that up to the "other" professionals. We are simply a source and guide to help you make positive changes.

Our book addresses the entire regulation process and uses reflection to set the stage for controlling emotions. It allows a passage to a more soothing, calming, and regulated breathing process. "Breathe" has been described in our book as the default method for self control and self regulation. As a parent, you are going to take the responsibility and have the presence of mind to teach your child what an out-of- control body feels and looks like versus a controlled one. Once you have accomplished this, you can take it to the next level and work toward helping your child learn how to self-regulate.

Our exercises will help you learn to use the body as a guide. You will help your child become aware of his or her breathing, pulse rate, skin temperature, face color, and or sweating and shaking. These signs may be subtle in a mini meltdown or very apparent in an all-out temper tantrum. You will highlight the outcome of the exercises by noting the difference between those actions and your child's reactions to stress and aversions. Your dedication will teach coping skills when your child is faced with adversities.

The third R is **Rules**, and we dedicated a lengthy chapter with specific explanations about how to create boundaries and structure within the household. Chapter Two (about mindfulness) and Chapter Three (about creating a positive environment) are the precursors to Chapter Six (about rules). In that chapter we discussed family meetings, as it is imperative that when you are making rules, the entire family is involved. A parent who makes the rules for the child, gives little sense or meaning to the actual rule breaking for the child. When children write their own rules, they write them from experience. Children are rule breakers, as this is how they learn right from wrong. Children are also very good at breaking rules and do so at times to gain desired attention from the adult. The adult complies with the child's rule breaking by giving negative attention to the child, and thus begins the vicious cycle of not being able to get ahead of cycle the of negativity.

Instead, we suggested that building a foundation of responsibility to self and others, mindfulness, imagery, breathing, and reflective practices actually aid in setting the stage for rule building. As the family gathers, each person cooperates, take turns speaking, shares discussion time, and writes rules that they broke. Responsibility and respectfulness are the first rules during the family meeting.

We have seen parents write rules pertaining to themselves, such as "no screaming or yelling when I am angry, limit anger responses, drink one cup of decaffeinated coffee to help my health, and find an extra Saturday and Sunday time for my children." Children have written rules that start with *no* as often as feasible, such as "No hitting and no back talk," and other rules, such as "Do homework after snack and school, listen the first time my parent asks me to do something," and so on and so forth. It's important that rules are clear and concise and leave no room for interpretation. Rules should be black and white and provide crystal-clear expectations.

The breath you take when you calm yourself under stress is the breath you will teach your child and family members to take when they become overreactive. When the word *breathe* is used on a regular basis, the child understands that "falling out" can be regulated and that she receives more attention for showing control and regulation than from having a meltdown. Meltdowns require a lot of energy from the child and take a lot of energy from the parents to combat. It is much easier to say "breathe," say it again if you must, and then move toward sighting what your child is changing in the way of self-control. Sometimes you will exaggerate a bit and build a mountain out of a molehill, but it's worth the little bit of exaggeration to keep the positive process moving forward.

Finally in Chapter Six we discussed the credit system. The credit system is unlike a typical token economy, in that the child loses points. Our credit system is forward moving, and the child can only gain points for jobs well done. These so-called jobs include positive changes in behavior, language changes, thought changes, and anything the parent feels should be rewarded. We do not advocate "buying" your child's behavior. Credits are given with you in control. Your child does not tell you when she should receive a credit, and credits are weaned in a short time, exchanging them for verbal rewards and physical hugs. So, as you give points or credits, you also give the long-term fix, which is verbal sightings, true praise, and positive emotions, as well as parent hugs and low and high fives.

Our examples range from house rules to chore charts to give you a sense of how to build structure. Your boundaries and rules come from this structure, and it is you who models behavior for your child. Some parents role-play social situations and problem solve together. Breathe, chatter or talk less, and sight with your new language more. Give kudos for the positive and little to no response other than "breathe" when it warrants it. Stay in neutral gear. This will keep your child wanting your positive attention. She will test and try to push you back to the negative, but hold your ground. Count to ten and breathe yourself. Practice your own self-regulation skills.

Traditional methods using consequences as punishment will "transition" to pseudo consequences and your child will retreat to the safe place and attempt to control herself. The more readily you accept your child taking a consequence in place and breathing with no punitive measures, the more attention will be given to the positive and the scale will tip in your favor.

Rubrics, the fifth R and last component in the step-by-step process, is one that you may decide to implement. As professionals working in school systems, we have used and seen teachers use rubrics to put the onus of learning on the student. We have come full circle and are right back to **Responsibility**, which we started at the beginning of this chapter and this book. Everything in between allows you to decide if you wish to try rubrics in your program. All the previous chapters have been influential in getting your child to regulate, and regulation leads to higher self-esteem, independence, confidence, achievement, and success.

> A rubric can be used for a systemic evaluation of self, or it can be used and designed for outside-the-box thinking.

The responsibility of learning which is initiated by the child, by using the rubric shows full evolution of behavior. It is hoped that by the time the child is ready to attempt to evaluate her social, academic, or behavioral performance, she will be regulated and will want to challenge her potential.

Rubrics are not negative, and they are not stressful, but what they are is something that can stimulate a child to challenge herself. The best challenge is that of self, as it makes one grow stronger, mature, and find their "center." By the time you as the parent have reached the point where you wish to try a rubric in your home, you will feel you have mastered the Student Empowerment Program© and the 5 Rs© and have seen the difference it has made in your family and household.

Here is something we found on the Internet that reminds us of a celebration of life! It is the rubric song from You Tube called "Phillip Glass Rubric," and it can be found at https://www.youtube.com/watch?v=hStHPRzmSWo.

SUMMARY

We shared a synopsis of our Student Empowerment Program© throughout this chapter. This new field guide will serve as a companion to our first book, *Early Childhood Education and the Student Empowerment Program©*. This field guide explores strategies and techniques and provides suggestions and activities for parents and other caregivers to use at home to help change unwanted behaviors and instill a positive climate in the household. We believe a child's first teachers are the parents. Hence, the parents' role is extremely important.

Self-regulation is important, too, as children are constantly faced with decision making, problem solving, and other challenges. Once your child understands how to monitor behavior, control emotions, and raise her self-esteem, she will understand empowerment.

Take it one step at a time, one moment at a time, and address what needs to be addressed. Learn to allow others to speak. Be a good listener. Learn how to keep moving forward while you take time to help a single soul. Take the time to teach your child how to avoid problems and practice breathing to decompress, and take the time to teach why lifelong learning is important. Every day assume the responsibility for the care of your child's brain. Reflect, regulate, create positive rules, and follow them consistently, fairly, and with consideration for each individual. And in the end, layer learning through rubrics to create self-dependent learners.

Bibliography

Allen, S. and Daly, K. (2002) "The Effects of Father Involvement: An Updated Research Summary of the Evidence." Retrieved at: https://library.parenthelp.eu/wp-content/uploads/2017/05/Effects_of_Father_Involvement.pdf.

Almendrala, Anna, (2017) "This Is Where Self-Esteem Lives in the Brain." Retrieved at: https://www.huffpost.com/entry/self-esteem-brain_n_5500501.

Barbiere, M. & Wiatr, J. (2020) *Early Childhood Education and the Student Empowerment Program,* Rowman and Littlefield, Lanham, MD.

Barbiere, M. (2018) *Setting the Stage: Delivering the Plan-Using the Learner's Brain Model* Rowman and Littlefield, Lanham, MD.

Barbiere, M. (2018) *Activating the Learners Brain Using the Learners Brain Model,* Rowman and Littlefield, Lanham, MD.

Brain Basics: "Anxiety Fight, Flight and Freeze Responses." Retrieved at: https://www.bing.com/videos/search?q=brain+exercise+for+flight+fight+or+fear&docid=6080228781376963O3&mid=228DBCB6F3DF7CCEA8E3228DBCB6F3DF7CCEA8E3&view=detail&FORM=VIRE.

Clark, C. (Jan 2007) "Why It Is Important to Involve Parents in Their Children's Literacy Development—a Brief Research Summary," National Literacy Trust. Retrieved at: https://files.eric.ed.gov/fulltext/ED496346.pdf.

Desforges, C. and Abouchaar, A. (2003) "The Impact of Parental Involvement, Parental Support and Family Education on Pupil Achievement and Adjustment: A Literature Review," 30. London: Department for Education and Skills.

Clark, N., Hatton-Bowers, H., Gottschals, C., Dev, and D. Poppe, L. (June 2017), "Self-Regulation in Early Childhood," NebGuide. Retrieved at: https://extensionpublications.unl.edu/assets/pdf/g2288.pdf.

Editorial Staff. (2023) "53 Interesting Facts about the Brain," 2023, The FACTfile. Retrieved at: https://thefactfile.org/brain-facts/3/.

Bibliography

Harlow, G. "Fun Facts About the Brain That Will Blow Your Mind," *The Legacy Blog.* Retrieved at: https://legacybox.com/blogs/analog/25-brain-facts-blow-mind.

Hart, B. and Risley, T. R. (1995) *Meaningful Differences in the Everyday Experience of Young American Children.* Paul H. Brookes Publishing, Washington, D.C.

Healthy Children Magazine, (Fall 2007) "What's Going on in the Teenage Brain?" Retrieved at: https://www.healthychildren.org/English/ages-stages/teen/Pages/Whats-Going-On-in-the-Teenage-Brain.aspx.

Jensen, Eric. (2005)Teaching with the Brain in MInd Rev 2nd edition, ASCD, Wasington, D.C.

"Kids Learning Style Survey, Love to Know." Retrieved at: https://cf.ltkcdn.net/kids/files/3923-Kids-Learning-Style-Survey.pdf.

Markowitz, K. and Jensen, E. (1999) *The Great Memory*, Corwin Press, Thousand Oaks, CA.

McLeod, S (2023). Piagets' Formal Ooperaional Statages:An Overivew & Examples. Retrieved at: https://www.simplypsychology.org/formal-operational.html.

Nunley, K. (2003) *A Student's Brain: The Parent/Teacher Manual.* Morris Publishing Kearney, NE.

Oariu, R. (October 26, 2021) "How to Handle Autism Meltdowns—Guide for Parents of Children with Autism." Retrieved at: https://spectrumdisorder.com/article/how-handle-autism-meltdowns-guide-parents-children-autism.

Price-Mitchell, M. "Motivational Quotes for Kids That Help Build Positive Relationships." Retrieved at: https://www.rootsofaction.com/motivational-quotes-kids/.

Silverstein, Shel. (2022) *21 Short and Sweet Shel Silverstein Poems That'll Bring You Back to Childhood.* Taken from *Where the Sidewalk Ends*, (1976). Retrieved at https://www.harpercollins.com/blogs/harperkids/shel-silverstein-poems.

Sousa, D. A. (2011) *How the Brain Learns* (4th ed.). Corwin Press, Thousand Oaks, CA.

Tamm, S. (2022) http: "Do Kids Really Need Routines and Schedules?" The Military Wife and Mom.

Taylor, L. "Tattling vs Reporting." Retrieved at: https://www.youtube.com/watch?v=1kwvkTcFDUM.

Urban Institute. (2012) "A Child's Home Environment Has a Long-Term Effect on Development." Retrieved at: http://www.urbanchildinstitute.org/sites/all/files/databooks/TUCI_Data_Book_VII_2012.05_family.pdf.

Weinberger, Evan (2022) "Staying Ahead of the Game—Self-Regulation vs. Self-Control—Staying Ahead of the Game (SAOTG)." Retrieved at: https://saotg.com/self-regulation-vs-self-control/.

White, J. (Spring 2020) "Using Rubrics and Self-Monitoring with Young Children." Northwestern College, Iowa NW Commons. Retrieved at: https://nwcommons.nwciowa.edu/cgi/viewcontent.cgi?article=1224&context=education_master.

Wong, M. (2014) "Stanford Study Finds Walking Improves Creativity." *Stanford News*. Retrieved at https://news.stanford.edu/2014/04/24/walking-vs-sitting-042414/.

Zakeri, M. and Karimoour, M. (2011) "Parenting Styles and Self-Esteem." *Procedia Social and Behavioral Sciences,* Vol., 29, pp. 758–61.

About the Authors

Dr. Mario C. Barbiere is a passionate practitioner with a strong theoretical background. Dr. Barbiere was a teacher, school administrator at all levels—assistant superintendent, superintendent, professor, and school turnaround specialist. He is committed to closing the achievement gap and providing positive student academic success. He worked at the district and state level for school turnaround, while promoting student self-regulation and empowerment. He has authored two books on brain research and lesson design and two books on brain research and instructional delivery based on his doctoral studies regarding educational neuroscience and practical experience in education.

Jane C. Wiatr is an early childhood education veteran, Intervention and Referral Services chairperson, 504 chairperson, and anti-bullying specialist in the State of New Jersey. Her experiences in pre-K Head Start and her many years in the early childhood classroom have served as the foundation for her strong early childhood philosophies. Jane believes in the social, emotional, and cognitive domains of learning through hands-on experiences. Play of all types is highly stressed in Jane's world. Self-regulation and -reflection, as well as nontraditional teaching methods are her forte, and she has proven this by teaching how to implement positive strategies and techniques to gain results. Jane began the first mainstreaming inclusion program in her district and began the first Alternate Route Program for pre-K through third grade for students at Kean University in New Jersey. Jane is a lifelong learner and continues to build skills by presenting workshops to parents and educators and offering private tutoring.

www.ingramcontent.com/pod-product-compliance
Lightning Source LLC
Chambersburg PA
CBHW030404170426
43202CB00010B/1489